To Ca

KEYS TO SUCCESS

Sir John Templeton

KEYS TO SUCCESS

50 SECRETS FROM A BUSINESS MAVERICK

JOHN TIMPSON

ICON

Published in the UK in 2017
by Icon Books Ltd, Omnibus Business Centre,
39–41 North Road, London N7 9DP
email: info@iconbooks.com
www.iconbooks.com

Sold in the UK, Europe and Asia
by Faber & Faber Ltd, Bloomsbury House,
74–77 Great Russell Street,
London WC1B 3DA or their agents

Distributed in the UK, Europe and Asia
by Grantham Book Services,
Trent Road, Grantham NG31 7XQ

Distributed in the USA
by Publishers Group West,
1700 Fourth Street, Berkeley, CA 94710

Distributed in Australia and New Zealand
by Allen & Unwin Pty Ltd,
PO Box 8500, 83 Alexander Street,
Crows Nest, NSW 2065

Distributed in South Africa
by Jonathan Ball, Office B4, The District,
41 Sir Lowry Road, Woodstock 7925

Distributed in Canada
by Publishers Group Canada,
76 Stafford Street, Unit 300
Toronto, Ontario M6J 2S1

ISBN: 978-178578-199-5

Typeset in Agmena Pro by Marie Doherty

Printed and bound in the UK
by Clays Ltd, St Ives plc

This book is dedicated to all the Timpson colleagues who make things happen. Twenty years ago we started to run the business by giving every colleague the authority to do their job in the way they know best. They have repaid that trust by creating a great business. I am proud to have played a small part in that success.

ABOUT THE AUTHOR

John Timpson CBE was born in 1943 and educated at Oundle and Nottingham University. In 1975 he became Managing Director of William Timpson Ltd, the business that had borne his family name since 1865, and he is now sole owner of the company, which has a turnover in the UK of £200m per year. His previous books include *Ask John* (Icon, 2014), based on his *Daily Telegraph* column of the same name, and *High Street Heroes* (Icon, 2015). His book *Upside Down Management* (Wiley, 2010) was described by the *Financial Times* as 'a practical and inspirational manual for anyone who runs a business'. Timpson and his late wife Alex were foster carers for 31 years, during which time they fostered 90 children. He lives in Cheshire.

Contents

Introduction

When I was asked to write this book I never realised how much it would teach me about our own business. It made me think. Before the book came into my life I'd never listed the most important elements of our management style. The list didn't take long to compile. On a wet afternoon on Mustique, when tennis was cancelled, it only took an hour to pick my top 50 management secrets. I emailed them to my son James who added four of his own and I already had the basis of this book.

It was only when I started to think about the detail that I began to learn more about the way we run our business. As I tackled each heading, describing how and why each element works, I was expecting to find it a tough task to find enough good reasons to support my faith in this maverick approach to management. But it strengthened my resolve to keep running our company 'upside down'.

I have been talking to conferences about 'Upside Down Management' for over fifteen years and hardly any delegates have had the courage to follow our example. Some will have found it impossible to persuade their boss to delegate and trust his workforce with the freedom to use their initiative, but I expect most thought I was an eccentric with an interesting idea that was OK for a small family-owned chain of cobblers, but wouldn't work for them.

My approach to management is probably defined by some of the things that aren't included in the list of contents. You won't find budgets, appraisals, big data, market research, psychometric testing or corporate planning away days. To me management is about people not process, it is an art not a science. One of the few things I remember from my university course in Industrial Economics is a definition of profit – 'the reward for taking risks'. The current emphasis on best practice and governance runs the danger of stifling initiative and failing to recognise that wealth is created by entrepreneurs not administrators.

I considered rating my top 50 business tips at the end of the book in order of importance, but as soon as I started the task I realised why it would be meaningless (but I have picked my top 25 phrases from the beginning of the chapters). All 50 tips are part of a coordinated approach – each one fits our company culture and contributes to our way of working, which I call Upside Down Management. We believe it is the people in our business who create our success; management's role is to give them all the support they need.

I believe it's an approach that can be applied to any business and the principles also have relevance to the public sector. Perhaps we can persuade our politicians to promote 'Upside Down Government' with the emphasis on giving business the support it needs rather than producing regulations that force us to tick boxes and tell us what to do.

Every tip in this book has made an important contribution to the Timpson business. They all come with my personal guarantee that they really do make a difference. But none works in isolation, they are part of a culture which depends on having a company full of positive personalities. We couldn't have developed our individual management style without being blessed with an amazing collection of personable and talented colleagues.

I hope this book transmits a bit of the buzz that I get every time I spend a day visiting our shops or chatting to colleagues in our offices and workshops. I also hope that it will convince other business leaders, and even some in government, that the best way to run an organisation is by picking a team of great personalities, trusting them with the authority to do their job in their own way and giving them all the support they need.

I am lucky to have a wholly-owned family business which seldom has borrowings and never has any interference from outside shareholders. This has given me the freedom to discover the huge benefits of running a business by using a combination of initiative, a bit of flair and, hopefully, a lot of common sense. If you are looking for some golden rules to create a great business you won't find them in the pages that follow. I don't like rules. If there is a magic formula it is to free the organisation from the constraints of the modern world, ignore regulations and process and be true to yourself by having the courage to be different. You will discover that by avoiding what others see as 'best practice' you will not only have more chance of success, everyone in the business will have a lot more fun.

1

Break the rules

If it doesn't feel right, don't do it.

Management is an art not a science; break the rules, but stick to your principles.

I am pleased that Nottingham University awarded me a Bachelor of Arts not Bachelor of Science when I completed my degree in Industrial Economics – management is an art not a science. This is much misunderstood throughout business, government and the public services where most managers do their job by following a process and sticking to their rules.

As a result, performance is measured by the ability to follow the process rather than concentrating on the ultimate objective. When recruiting, it doesn't matter if you pick a poor candidate as long as you follow the proper interview process. Ofsted can withdraw an 'outstanding' rating from an amazingly good school simply because a bit of the paperwork is missing. Our well established and highly successful Timpson apprenticeship scheme doesn't qualify for any government grants because there isn't an NVQ for cobblers. Young doctors get disillusioned with the NHS because they have invisible bosses who are policing a process that soaks up time that should be spent caring for patients.

As C. Northcote Parkinson predicted, it is getting worse. Organisations become an end in themselves, building a bigger team that spends their time devising rules to tell other people how to do a job they don't do themselves. Beware any organisation that uses the phrases 'evidence-based', 'joined-up thinking', 'working party' or 'in-depth study'.

We really don't have to put up with all the rules that get in the way of doing our day-to-day business. Business leaders only have themselves to blame for allowing lawyers, accountants and so-called 'professional managers' to dictate that the only way we can do business is by sticking to the rules and following what they consider to be best practice.

I didn't realise how bad things have become until we took

part in a government procurement process in connection with the proposal to introduce biometric passports.

We were naive, thinking all that mattered was our ability to provide future passport holders with a great service in capturing the new data. But the process was run under strict EU guidelines which eliminated any chance of a company as small as ours competing. It was all done online, no one wanted to see who we are or what we do – the winner was bound to be the team that picked professional advisors, who proved to be the best at following the process. We fell at the first hurdle, but it all came to an end with a change of government. Biometric passports were abandoned, every bidder had to put their hard work down to experience, but the professionals still picked up their fees. What a waste of time, money and talent.

I've always been a bit of a maverick, keen to stand my ground when authority flies in the face of common sense. Many times I've been told 'You can't do that', a remark that makes me even more determined to do it my way. I got a lot of cautionary advice when we were introducing Upside Down Management. 'You can't let each shop charge what they want – you have to have a price list.' 'I have a price list', I replied, 'and I let each shop charge what they want.' I have had similar debates over our approach to poor performers who we politely and generously ask to leave without the pedantic production of oral and written warning. 'You must find yourself in lots of employment tribunals', I'm told, but we don't, because we treat our colleagues as human beings rather than part of a process.

I was inspired in this determined quest to ignore perceived best practice and follow my instincts by my wife Alex, whose allergy to process was so acute she never stayed in a meeting for more than an hour. Alex saw way beyond the daily constraints of form-filling (which I had to do on her behalf) and budgeting (she never looked at her bank account). By keeping clear of the conventional ways of business, Alex had a vivid view of the big picture, and a perceptive insight into people's personality. Alex could never understand why businesses needed to compile long reports or hold meetings that lasted longer than an hour. While most of the world made things more complicated, Alex simply used a bit of intuition and a lot of common sense. Give me inspired instinct rather than measured process every time.

My maverick mood was strengthened by a breakfast meeting with Judith Hackitt CBE, then Chief Executive of the Health and Safety Executive. Our meeting was the result of an article I wrote in my *Telegraph* column about silly Health and Safety regulations that get companies to spend extra money when they should be making individual colleagues more responsible for their own safety. I found that Judith and I were in total agreement and we went on to talk about PAT testing of electrical equipment. Over breakfast with Judith, I discovered there is no legal requirement: PAT tests are entirely voluntary. I checked with Michelle (the sole member of our Health and Safety department), who confirmed it to be true – no statute talks about PAT testing, it is just the safety consultants who say it is the only way to make sure you are compliant. Michelle went on to tell me that over two years none of our PAT tests (at a cost of £40,000) had revealed a fault – every electrical problem had been discovered and reported by our own colleagues. We now only carry out the tests in shops where the landlord makes it a condition of the lease.

Another, even more bizarre procedure that businesses thought they had to follow, was created in the 1960s when, every fortnight, two women came to our office to clean and disinfect our telephones. They kept coming for years before anyone realised it was a complete waste of money. It's satisfying to know that we are not the first generation to fall for these snake oil salesmen.

It is particularly frustrating when you come up against silly rules you can't break, like the security inspection at Fenchurch Street station. Our tiny shop had an open front with a space no more than 3ft × 6ft between the counter and the pavement. Every retailer at the station had to inspect their customer area every hour and sign a form to confirm nothing suspicious had been found. A security guy called every hour to check we had filled in the form. One day our shop colleague had to leave the shop to pick up some shoes from a customer and missed checking the 18 square feet and failed to tick the 10.00am box, so the station manager punished us by shutting the shop for the rest of that day. As the branch didn't make much money, we solved the problem by shutting the shop for good.

Some of the most stupid rules have been created by employment lawyers who seem to think that there is absolutely no difference between one person and another. Alex was on the interview panel for a new head at our local primary school and came to me with a copy of all the application forms. 'But they don't tell me what I want to know', she said. 'I don't know anything about these people – age, sex, home background and everything I would be interested in is missing from their application form and to make it worse they all seem to say exactly the same thing about why they should be given the job.' To avoid being accused of discrimination we are in danger of discriminating in favour of people who would be no good at the job.

A lot of this modern day 'best practice' has been fashioned

by accountants, lawyers and consultants, who can be called the rules creation and exploitation sector. Every new bit of legislation brings a new round of breakfast seminars at which professional firms tell us how to keep within the new laws while enhancing their fee income. Don't you cringe whenever someone stops you in the street to ask 'Have you had an accident at work?' By finding a new source of income, lawyers and insurance companies put up the cost of running every other business.

By now you must have guessed that I take a certain pleasure in breaking the rules, but I do so with a purpose. Entrepreneurs make money by using their initiative and being different. If you tread the same path and follow the same process as everyone else you won't stand out from the crowd and can never create a great business.

We must be the only major retailer that refuses to use EPOS (electronic point of sale), but by denying our central support team the chance of being in total control, we have given our branch colleagues the freedom to give great service. By having the courage to do it in our own way, we have managed to establish a level of customer care that is starting to stand out from other retailers.

The way most companies now do business reminds me of the story of the emperor's suit of clothes. No one seems to have the courage to blow the whistle on all the process and best practice or see through the plastic world of box-ticking. Be like the little boy who saw the truth – bold business leaders see through convention and follow their convictions. If it doesn't feel right, don't do it.

Upside Down Management

This is the big idea that made us much more money and established a strong company culture.

Upside Down Management is great for colleagues' wellbeing.

W hen I started to read *The Nordstrom Way*, written about the eponymous American chain of department stores, I didn't realise that it was going to make such a massive difference to the way we run our business.

The book reveals the secret behind great customer service. Most companies get it wrong. You can't create great service simply by writing a set of rules, not much is achieved by inventing friendly phrases designed to impress customers, and customer care training courses seldom give the customers the sort of service that will make them go 'Wow'. The secret is so obvious and so simple, I'm embarrassed to admit that I was running our company for over 21 years before I got the message.

The secret is to trust your colleagues with the freedom to serve each individual customer in the best way they can. Exceptional service, when colleagues sometimes literally go the extra mile, usually occurs when the customer has an unusual request, something that can't be covered by a set of rules. Nordstrom gave their front-line sales clerks total authority to use their initiative, and they did something else that made a big impression on me. In the middle of the book was a management chart that was upside down. The people who served the customers were up at the top and the chief executive was right at the bottom. The sales clerks are top of the tree because they do the key job that makes the money; everyone else in the company is there to help and support their colleagues on the front line.

Upside Down Management suddenly seemed to me such an obvious thing to do. As a manager who couldn't repair shoes or cut a key I had, for years, been reliant on colleagues, working in our shops, to do the jobs that made us the money. I was never in a position to tell them what to do, so it seemed far better to abandon the traditional management methods of command and control and concentrate on giving front-line colleagues trust and support.

As soon as I got the message, I was on a mission to turn our management structure upside down, but it took a long time to persuade the rest of my business. Shop colleagues, who I thought would welcome the freedom on offer, were reticent and most of middle management totally disagreed with the whole idea.

The people in our shops were so used to following our rule book that they didn't believe I was seriously going to give them the freedom to do whatever they wanted. And those that thought it was a good idea were wary of their area managers who had always kept rigid control.

Recognising that people like to have some rules, I just had two: 1) Look the part; 2) Put the money in the till. But to emphasise the degree of trust, I added two guidelines: 1) Anyone, even a new recruit in their first week, can spend up to £500 to settle a complaint, without reference to anyone else; 2) The price list is only a guide – you can charge whatever you think is the appropriate price.

Gradually shop colleagues got the message, but it took me nearly five years to get our area managers to let go. It was difficult to stop them issuing orders. 'How can I be responsible for the results of my area', they argued, 'if I can't tell anyone what to do?' Some feared for their job – 'If I hand over the authority for everything to members of my team, what will be left for me to do?' I wrote a manual about their new role and we discussed it, section by section, at area manager conferences spread over a period of nearly three years. Gradually some area managers got it and became enthusiastic, while a few uncooperative managers moved on to different roles. It isn't surprising it took so long to change their attitude; culture change doesn't happen overnight.

Once our area managers were persuaded, they suddenly realised that their new job was so much better than the old one. Instead of dreaming up all the rules and telling everyone what to do, they now have the time to pick the right people, put them together in strong teams and clear away any obstacles in the way of them doing a great job. With many of those obstacles being problems that occur outside work, our area managers now find that providing a sort of social service is an important part of their job.

Originally I saw Upside Down Management as a way of providing a better service by giving trust and freedom to the front line, but now I know that everyone in the organisation should be trusted to do their job in the way they want. Managers can run their department in their own way as long as they give the same freedom to all the members of their team. The principle even applies to me – I can't issue orders but I don't have to follow anyone else's rules. I might have to comply with the law but there is no need for me to follow 'best practice'. Like everyone else who works at Timpson I do my job in my own way.

We started Upside Down Management in 1998 and it has worked better with every year that goes by. There are many reasons why it has been so successful. For a start it makes you pick people with a great personality – it soon became clear that dull and pedestrian characters don't use their initiative. In addition, the business has become bristling with ideas created by colleagues with the freedom to do their own thing. Most of all, our colleagues enjoy coming to work.

Colleagues really like being trusted, they take a pride in running a shop they feel they can call their own. They value the freedom to make decisions and the support they get from a boss who doesn't issue any orders. When we acquired the Morrisons dry cleaning business in June 2016, the colleagues who transferred to Timpson were amazed that we have such a relaxed approach to business with so few rules and so much freedom.

I wasn't surprised when a psychologist, who had made a study of the power of delegation, told me that having the freedom to be in control of your working life is very good for employees' wellbeing. Perhaps that's why I find it such fun visiting our shops and meeting so many colleagues with a smile on their face. I will never forget the comment from a colleague who joined us when we bought the business where he was working. 'I was worried at first', he told me, 'but after two years I am amazed how much my life has changed. I now look forward to coming to work and I also look forward to going home, where my wife says I'm more relaxed and much better company.' There is no doubt that a happy workforce will produce better results – another reason why Upside Down Management is so good for business.

But there is another big benefit. When you have established an upside down culture and no longer issue any orders you will find that the business is much easier to run. You no longer have to create a set of standing orders, there is no need to devise a process for everyone to follow. With no rules, your management team don't have to spend their time checking that everyone is following company policy. By giving every colleague the freedom to do their job in a way that suits them, managers can concentrate on the things that matter – choosing the right strategy, picking people with personality and giving them the support they need to put the strategy into practice.

I promise you it works and it must be the easiest way to run a business.

Trust your people

Businesses that are paranoid about theft and security create a negative atmosphere, stifle initiative, prevent proper personal service and undermine company loyalty.

If you can't trust your colleagues you must be picking the wrong people.

I've never understood why so many companies run their business in a way that is primarily designed to thwart the 5 per cent of their workforce who may be dishonest. Organisations go to great lengths to make all transactions totally secure, plugging every possible weakness in their system and, in doing so, produce a detailed control process that strips all the honest colleagues of the chance to use their initiative for the good of the business and its customers.

Although we at Timpson keep a realistic eye wide open, I believe in trusting every colleague. Life is so much easier and the workplace happier if you presume everyone is honest. It is demeaning to people who are subjected to strict security guidelines that presume, given the chance, every colleague will pinch the company's money. I felt uncomfortable when watching the staff at one supermarket, as they were obliged to open their personal bags for inspection every time they left for home.

This is an example of how a heavy-handed process gets in the way of proper management. Many of the rules are there to cover the management's back ahead of the next episode of financial loss. Some claim secure systems are required for insurance purposes, and there have been court cases that suggest employers have a duty to take temptation as far away from their employees as possible. But in my experience theft is best detected and controlled by understanding what is going on every day, knowing your colleagues and keeping a close interest in the day-to-day business. At Timpson we still catch someone thieving almost every week but our total loss through internal theft has dropped significantly since we relied on trust rather than regulations. Companies are continually introducing new systems to stop the latest dishonest ploy but they will never be able to stop the determined thief finding another route to pinching money.

I never cease to be amazed at the lengths some people will go to beat the system. One of my favourite scams occurred in Scotland in the 1970s. At that time Tuf shoes with their six-month guarantee were, at 42/9 (about £2.14), the biggest selling men's shoe and were stocked by nearly every value shoe chain in the country, including Timpson and Freeman, Hardy & Willis (FHW). In a town south of Glasgow the managers of the Timpson and FHW shops came to an arrangement. Just before the annual stocktaking was due to take place at the Timpson branch the manager 'borrowed' all the FHW stock of Tuf shoes to enhance the value of his total stock and cover up some of the takings that had slipped into his pocket. Once the stock auditor had moved on to his next assignment the FHW manager got his shoes back with a promise that he would take care of the Timpson stock of Tuf shoes in time for his next stocktake.

Another bizarre and brazen scam took place in a competitor's shop in south-east England. The shop had two employees, but if anyone went to call they would find only one of them. Visitors were told that the other colleague was on his day off, but in truth he was running their own independent shop down the road. This multiple competitor wasn't just paying the wages of someone to run their own business, the crafty couple also ordered extra materials and spare machinery parts that allowed them to trade almost cost-free in their little shop round the corner.

I'm not proposing a totally naive approach that believes dishonesty doesn't exist – there will always be someone trying to take a financial advantage, even if you think you have closed every loophole. Sometimes, when visiting one of our shops I sense that something is wrong. There are some significant signals: the shop manager who has beads of sweat on his brow and can't look you in the eye, sales figures that shoot up when a mobile colleague covers for the manager's holiday, shops that look busier than the takings suggest and a manager full of excuses to explain the lack of trade.

True confidence in your colleagues isn't just about trusting them to put the money in the till – it also includes trusting everyone with the freedom to use their initiative rather than insisting that every job is done according to rigid standing orders. I got a little hint of the culture that exists in some parts of the NHS when I met a management consultant who had been asked to study a number of hospital trusts. 'I had a big problem', he told me, 'the one that performed best against the NHS targets came bottom of the pile when it came to having happy and satisfied patients.' Sticking to the rules might bring better ratings at your next appraisal but you can't create a company with personality by laying down strict rules.

A good barometer of culture and management style is the company complaints policy. Process-driven organisations have a comprehensive system that controls the handling of complaints. Colleagues in the front line aren't trusted with the authority to sort out any problem, however trivial. Any exchange of goods or compensation payout must have the blessing of their line manager who probably needs to talk to the boss who in turn must get permission in writing from Head Office.

The result of this complex complaint chain of command is a collection of unhappy customers (who are now more irritated about the delay than the original complaint) and an overworked and very busy complaints department at the office. I know from experience that trusting your colleagues to take responsibility can save a lot of money.

We seem to live in a world full of suspicion, where no one is to be trusted. Everyone believes it is necessary to follow rules set down by the government, Health and Safety officers, insurance companies, the finance director, lawyers, accountants and the HR department. Too many people now believe that good managers are measured by their ability to make everyone in the organisation stick to the process. I totally disagree – the truly great executives set the strategy, have the charisma to create a positive culture and give their talented colleagues the space to do their own thing.

I hope by now you are getting my message. If you don't trust your employees they are highly unlikely to trust their customers. About twenty years ago, B&Q, the DIY chain, had a reputation for poor service. There was a good reason: shop colleagues were told that their most important job was to stop customers pinching the stock. They did as they were told, every customer was watched carefully and observed with single-minded suspicion. Stock shrinkage shrank but so did the sales. A move to customer-friendly, more mature sales people made a massive difference to sales without increasing the amount of theft.

Retailers, who fear that every other customer is a threat rather than an opportunity, set several rules to keep the consumer in check. 'No £50 notes.' 'We don't accept credit cards for payment below £10.' 'No refund without a receipt.' And 'Only three school children inside the shop at the same time!'

My dream is to have shop colleagues who are so trusted they have the confidence to give £10 to say sorry to a customer whose key doesn't work; and if someone who has lost their wallet or purse is collecting a shoe repair, to have the sense to say, 'No problem, take the shoes now and pay me when you're next near my shop.'

It gives the business a massive boost if you trust your colleagues. Trust their honesty, trust their diligence – timekeeping, determination and loyalty – and trust their judgement. If you can't trust your colleagues you must be picking the wrong people.

Only two rules

---✂---

*The more rules you have, the less
important they become.*

**If you could only have two
rules, what would they be?**

In 1995, just after we bought the Automagic chain of shoe repair shops, I was visiting their branch in the Metro Centre, Gateshead, where I saw an innovative display of shoe polish, so I produced my camera and took a photo. 'I'm sorry', said the manager, looking sheepish, 'I'll put it back to the standard layout straight away.' He thought I'd taken the picture to prove he hadn't followed company instructions.

Before our takeover Automagic had been run with a rod of iron by a dictatorial management who expected their word to be obeyed, so it's not surprising that the Gateshead manager was concerned when I caught him stepping out of line. To be honest, a few years earlier the Timpson business was pretty much the same, with area managers tasked with making sure that every shop worker complied with the *Standing Orders for Shoe Repair Factories* which set out our rules in meticulous detail, emphasised on bold notices pinned up in the staff area of every store.

That conversation in the Metro Centre made me realise how much we had changed. My management style was always less military and more casual than the traditional system of command and control but we still had all the old rules. It was time for a change and, as noted earlier, I decided to scrap the standing orders and replace them with two simple rules: 1) Look the part; 2) Put the money in the till.

I chose these two rules because they highlight the essentials of shopkeeping. I can't contemplate a shop being successful if scruffy staff turn up late to a messy branch and seldom put the takings in the till. These things really matter, but I am happy for branch colleagues to change our displays or dress up and have a fun day. If they think that they know a better way to increase sales, why not let them have a go?

Every other rule was scrapped. We stopped telling everyone how to do their job and pleaded with them to use their new-found freedom to follow their initiative. But they were still bemused, worried that their local boss would be unhappy if they followed the new company policy. So, to emphasise my point, I published two guidelines: 1) You can spend up to £500 to settle a customer complaint without referring to anyone else – no need to call the area manager or Head Office, just do it yourself. 2) Charge what you want – treat our price list as a guide but feel free to charge each customer the price you think is right. At last they started to get the message and used our trust to give their customers a better service.

Most multiple retailers have standard window displays and the stock layout is rigidly controlled with a planagram, laying down exactly what goes where. We aren't bothered – in fact we tell our colleagues if they want to paint their shop pink that's fine by us (our Max Spielmann shop in Faversham was painted pink but sadly sales stayed the same). I don't visit shops to nitpick, I am not there to catch people out or tell them what to do. Because they are free from stifling rules I can look for the ideas that are produced by their initiative.

The only time I complain during a shop visit is when I see that one of the rules is being broken. It is difficult to spot people breaking rule 2 about putting the money in the till, but any suspicion is relayed to our security department. However, it's pretty obvious when a colleague breaks rule 1. If I arrive to find the shop shut, spot sloppy housekeeping or meet a colleague with stubble but without a tie in a shop full of rubbish, I have to criticise – walking off without comment isn't an option. My two rules help us focus on the things that really make a difference.

I urge all organisations to do something similar. Over time the size of every rule book increases – look at the rules of golf. It takes over 30,000 words to regulate a game that simply entails hitting a ball into a hole. Successive governments pass new laws to put their policies into practice and pass many more to shut the stable door on the causes of the latest scandal, in every area of life from business fraud to child neglect.

Lawyers, accountants and consultants make further additions to our national rule book by supporting each new regulation with guidelines and recommendations that gullible and risk-averse managers mistake for rigid regulations. This gold plating of the law has engulfed companies in so many rules that the main role of management is now seen as making sure all employees toe the line. The key business objectives of turnover, profit and cashflow become of considerably less importance.

The reality is even worse. With so many rules to follow, the operating team cannot keep up with every regulation. So, to satisfy regulators like Ofsted and the Ministry of Work and Pensions they concentrate on the paperwork, making sure all the policies are approved and complete records are kept on file. It doesn't matter if you break the rules, as long as the proper safeguards are in place.

I am particularly irritated by businesses that cover their backs by devising a set of rules for customers. I once went to a pub near Mobberley in Cheshire where the beer garden was peppered with signs telling customers what they could, and couldn't, do. 'All diners must leave a credit card behind the bar'; 'Children cannot use the slide unless a responsible adult is within 6 feet'; 'All breakages must be paid for', and many more. When I went to visit an aunt in Northampton General Hospital, I picked the wrong car park and had to walk down about half a mile of corridors to reach her ward. Every few yards was a notice giving me orders. 'Always walk on the left'; 'Strictly no entry'; 'Wash your hands before entering' – all following Health and Safety precautions, but there's a limit to how many orders a man can take. Since we appointed an active Health and Safety Committee at Delamere Forest Golf Club the number of warning signs has increased ten-fold, including 'Slippery Slope Ahead' and 'Don't drive off until you hear the bell', an instruction that is difficult to follow if there is no one else on the course.

As a result of all this regulation, most people think that there is a guideline to cover everything everyone does. This is why, on many occasions, when I show a bit of initiative, col-leagues tell me 'You can't do that!' But I won't be told. I have a simple test: if the supposed regulation simply isn't common sense, I do it my way. Even people from other companies who understand what I mean, still feel bound to follow the instruc-tions of the most risk-averse lawyer and claim: 'It's all right for you, you're a private company.'

My challenge to every organisation is to reduce all their rules to just two. The exercise makes them think about what really matters. I have seen the benefits at Delamere C of E Primary Academy, where Headteacher Steve Docking took little notice of the policies handed down by the local author-ity and simply concentrated on making the school a safe and welcoming place that provides children with a great educa-tion. By using these two objectives to guide every member of staff, Steve has turned his school into a centre of excellence for others to follow.

I even think there are probably two rules that would help to dramatically improve the NHS. My two rules would be: 1) Never put hygiene, health or safety at risk; 2) Do all you can to look after your patients.

What two rules would work in your business?

No one issues orders

─────── ❧ ───────

*It's devilishly difficult to get middle
management to delegate authority
while keeping responsibility – most
managers do it the other way round.*

**It is very tough running a
business by dictating the detail.**

Most people assume that managers should spend most of their time behind a desk, telling people what to do. It took me over five years to change that culture at Timpson. From the outset I declared that no one must issue instructions, but it takes patience to change the habits of a lifetime. The key to creating a belief in delegation at Timpson depended on our area managers. Their central role, conducting day-to-day business out in the field, meant they had a major influence on the attitude of our branch colleagues. Most of our area managers resisted the change.

They had been brought up in a company run by command and control. They all started on the shop floor and spent their formative years obeying their bosses' orders to the letter. Timpson had a strict set of rules in a booklet labelled *Standing Orders for Shoe Repair Factories*. After promotion, a new area manager got a car, clipboard and briefcase which he took from shop to shop making sure everyone was sticking rigidly to the standing orders.

It was a great shock when I abolished most of the rules and announced that, in future, the right way to run their area was to trust team members with the freedom to do their job the way they wanted. It was a massive change, as they weren't even delegating to the two or three deputies in their area team, who, like everyone else, did as they were told and spent most of their time filling in for branch managers who were on holiday or off sick.

As I have mentioned above, the area managers put up some strong resistance. 'How can I be responsible for the results of my area if I can't tell anyone what to do?' they said. And, when I suggested they should pass over parts of their role to their deputies, including training and staff cover for holidays and sickness,

I was met with the plea: 'If I hand over those jobs, what will be left for me to do?'

I wrote a training manual, using my usual format of lots of pictures and very few words, to describe their job in my Upside Down Management world. The team discussed my new guidelines bit by bit at a series of area conferences spread over three years. Some of the team found the concept too tough to take. It was clear when talking to colleagues as I visited their shops that they still expected everyone to stick to the old rules. Inevitably a few stepped down from area management but others got the message and discovered that this new role, far from being a backward step, made the job of management much more interesting.

It is very hard to do your job by dictating the detail. As soon as you take away the right to issue orders, managers find that they have to create success by picking the right people and giving them all the support they need. There is no need for the manager to feel, as some do, that they must know more than anyone else about everyone's job, just because they are the boss. It is a strength not a weakness to know your limitations and an invaluable management tool to recognise the things that team members do much better than you.

If the boss always runs the business by telling people what to do, there is only one person who is influencing decisions. Delegate freedom to all your colleagues and you suddenly benefit from everyone's initiative. By trusting your people you empower the business and make full use of the talent throughout your team.

Pick people with personality

Great companies have great people.

**Have a business full of characters
who rate 9 or 10 out of 10.**

W hen we introduced Upside Down Management we soon discovered it only works with the right people.

For decades we had got it wrong. We were hiring shoe repairers and key cutters when we should have been looking for people with personality. You can teach someone with character how to repair shoes but you can't put personality into a grumpy cobbler.

Success seems to come to people with charisma. We want more people like Bob who runs our shop in Taunton, Andy who is a well-known character on the Kings Road, Chelsea, P.J. who manages our shop in a cut-through in Reading called Smelly Alley, and Sue who runs our Max Spielmann business and spreads her enthusiasm round more than 350 shops.

We needed a way to persuade everyone involved in our recruitment process to judge applicants on their personality. I found the answer on a train from Crewe to Euston in 1995. I was with my son Edward, who at that time was studying to be a barrister. Before we reached London we had drafted our first Mr Men interview form, a series of pictures which included Mrs Happy, Mr Keen, Mr Punctual and Mr Helpful together with Mr Scruffy, Mr Dull, Mrs Slow and Ms Late. Under each picture is an empty box.

The form is easy to use – the interviewer simply ticks the boxes that best describe the person in front of them. It works! We don't bother much about CVs or the stories told on an application form. We certainly don't use psychometric testing, as the Mr Men pictures tell us all we need to know. To make sure, every candidate that passes the test spends a day in a branch working alongside one of our existing colleagues, which is time enough to confirm whether we have picked the right sort of person.

After many years of seeing the benefits that come from

recruiting for personality we decided to take things a stage further by starting to rate everyone out of 10. There is no science to this, we don't like appraisals, and it isn't part of a process, but we have discovered that most colleagues can instinctively rate their workmates' personality on a scale of 1 to 10. In 2011 we vowed to create a business exclusively made up of people who rate either a 9 or a 10 out of 10. It made a big difference, not only because we were full of positive personalities, but also because they very much appreciated working with colleagues with a similar outlook on life.

There is no doubt that 9s and 10s like to be part of a team full of other proactive characters. They certainly don't want to be surrounded by colleagues who regularly throw sickies, turn up late, do as little as they can get away with and spend much of the day looking at their iPhone.

Some will never qualify as a 9 or 10 – indeed there are plenty of workers who would be lucky to be rated 3 or 4. These are the people who think they are owed a job and have the right to take a selfish attitude. They aren't reliable, can't be trusted, don't care about customers, have no interest in the company performance and could never be described as team players. But you meet these people every day, in supermarkets, motorway service stations, on the high street and behind a reception desk.

Perhaps the companies that offer jobs to a 3 or a 4 don't realise what a difference they could make by raising their standards. Perhaps they are so driven by process that they control the wage cost and the head count without meeting the people who are on the payroll. Many companies carry out cost-cutting schemes by reducing the total number of part-time hours without thinking which part-timers should have their hours cut.

We interview about twelve applicants for every one that qualifies as a 9 or a 10. You have to wonder where our rejects find a job.

Raising the bar by simply aiming for 9s and 10s made a massive difference, because it stopped us picking the 7s and 8s. Those that rate 5 and below were quite definitely not for us, while a 7 or 8 was previously regarded as 'She's just about OK' or 'He'll do', but if you want a great business 'OK' isn't OK. You will never have a complete collection of great colleagues if you open your doors to Mr and Mrs Average.

Some years ago a company was taken to an employment tribunal because they advertised for hard-working people, the claim being that they were discriminating against those that didn't work hard. If that is illegal I'm happy to be guilty. We don't discriminate on the grounds of race, sex or disability, and we positively discriminate in favour of people leaving prison, but we will only pick people with personality.

A business full of 9s and 10s creates an incredible culture. It has a competitive buzz without energy being wasted on politics. People do it now, they don't spend time looking for reasons why it can't be done, and they love the challenge of new ideas. The team is at ease with itself and feels free to have fun.

Even better, a company full of personality will attract more 9s and 10s. As long as you keep high standards, recruitment will no longer be a problem. By filling the company full of great people you are well on the way to creating a great business.

Encourage flexible working

—— ⋈ ——

*The best results are produced by people whose
work fits in with the rest of their lives.*

**Flexible working is an important
part of trust, wellbeing and
Upside Down Management.**

When I started work in 1960 everyone who worked in our office had to clock in at 9.00am and clock out at 5.00pm, while the warehouse workers started an hour earlier. I was lucky – five years before I started work, the office still operated every Saturday morning. The only time anyone was missing from their desk was when they took their two weeks' annual holiday.

Technology, employment law and attitudes have changed a lot, but many companies have failed to keep up. In our modern world, old-fashioned workplaces find it harder to attract the best talent because they expect every employee to stick to tradition and follow the rules of a 9–5 culture. If you want the best person for the job, be prepared to fashion the role around their lifestyle. Don't expect them to totally change their life to suit the business.

Our office today is very different. Many people start at 7.30am and leave not long after lunch and some seldom come to the office at all – they can just as easily work at home, but we like to see them from time to time so that they keep in touch with rest of the team. Some turn up late on the days they take their children to school and others have a long lunch hour to do some shopping or go out jogging.

By being flexible we have a better chance of attracting the best people. It is more important to get colleagues who do a great job in their own way than to limit recruitment to people who are happy working to a rigid set of rules. Having a reputation for flexible working means we are much less likely to miss out on potential superstars.

There are many different ways in which we can help colleagues achieve their work–life balance. Some can only work part-time, others need to work from home, job sharing can be very successful and there are those who start and finish at unusual hours. We can also help by having a flexible approach to holidays and extended periods of absence, not just for childcare, but also sabbaticals, study leave and even, as has happened with us, an international amateur athlete who is training for a major championship.

Flexible working isn't just for women. Dads as well as mums may need to spend more time at home and plenty of people are committed carers. It doesn't matter whether the different work pattern is required to fulfil a role at home, attendance at college, practice sessions for a sports team or rehearsals for a drama group – the key requirement is getting the job done.

To successfully introduce flexible working the chief executive needs to create a feeling of trust throughout the organisation. It doesn't work if office-based workers suspect that colleagues who work from home are getting away with an easy life. The culture must concentrate on results rather than procedure. It doesn't matter where, when or how the work is done, we are only bothered about the end result.

Despite the legislation that covers flexible working it's nonsense to follow rigid rules. Any new arrangement should start with a conversation to establish whether there is a better way for the colleague to work, while still fulfilling their role in the business. There has to be a consensus: no one has the right to work in the way that suits them without making sure that it fits in with the business and their colleagues. That said, a successful flexible workplace will do everything possible to accommodate individual circumstances.

There is a limit. It is much easier to employ flexible workers in our offices compared with the shops. We have to be open for business during all the hours our customers want to go shopping, so branch-based colleagues can't work when the shops are shut and they certainly can't work from home. But we still have a lot of flexibility in the way rotas are organised. We know who likes working Sundays, who needs the bonus and is happy to do a six-day week and those that always spend every other Friday with their children.

Although I have already made clear that flexible working is just as important to men as women, it is a significant part of the drive to give women total equality in the workplace. For three years I was a member of the Women's Business Council where I actively promoted flexible working, but I always felt uneasy about the way the role of women in the workplace was given priority over the rest of their lives. Free childcare and pressure on women to stand up for their gender by seeking a seat in the boardroom may come at a price.

I support the thought that mums should be given every chance to have a career. A career break that goes beyond statutory maternity leave, when mums stay at home until their children are at full-time school, should not stand in the way of future promotion. As a foster carer I have seen the consequences of an early childhood that lacks the normal bond between parents and child. It is a complicated and emotional subject and my views may be unpopular with professional businesswomen who are keen to see more women at the top of businesses. But I think that, whoever you are, your family comes first and every mum and dad should be aware that their children need plenty of their time and lots of love. A significant percentage of teenagers who show challenging behaviour have attachment problems caused by a lack of bonding in the earliest years of their life.

Flexible working isn't just a good way to give working mums

the chance to do two jobs at the same time – it is good news for everyone. Upside Down Management trusts colleagues to do things their way. Flexible working takes this a stage further by giving them the chance to fit work into their lives instead of having to fit their lives around work. This must help to reduce stress, and I am convinced that flexible working is a major contributor to personal wellbeing.

In twenty years, flexible working will be the norm. We are already starting to think about running parts of our business without a formal office. More time for the family, less time spent commuting, and all the emphasis on what is achieved rather than how, where or when it is done. But (and it is an important but), we still need to meet up. Teams can't be totally remote. My two rules for flexible working are:

1. Do the job.
2. Meet the rest of the team at least once a month.

Say goodbye to drongos

———※———

Over 80 per cent of management time is spent dealing with people who make little or no contribution to the company's success. The only sensible thing to do is to say goodbye as nicely, as generously and as quickly as possible.

Every time a weak colleague leaves, you strengthen the business.

Recruiting people with the right personality is usually regarded as an executive's most important job, but saying goodbye to colleagues who are below standard matters just as much.

Weeding out poor performers is particularly important after an acquisition, especially if the new recruits have been part of a poor-performing business. Most businesses we have bought were making a loss and lots of the talented managers had long since departed to work for a more successful company. Consequently we inherited mediocre management teams who were happy to struggle along with the help of a below average workforce. In these circumstances it is wise to exercise a bit of patience. Don't implement a round of redundancies before talking to as many colleagues as possible and getting to know the business. Two tips: put one of your own people in charge and get to know the middle managers. There will be a few star performers hidden below the radar just waiting for the chance to work for an inspirational leader. Before long your patience will be rewarded, you will identify the weak links and start to make the personnel changes that are desperately needed.

It's relatively easy to say goodbye to a drongo who is part of an acquisition, but every business, however good they think they are, employs a few drongos who, if allowed to linger, will lower standards. We pride ourselves on our interview technique at Timpson but it isn't perfect, and some seemingly fantastic recruits turn out to be a big disappointment. It is important to make sure that these drongos don't cause any long-term damage to our reputation.

Before going any further I must define a drongo (Australian slang referring to a racehorse in the 1920s called Drongo that ran in 37 races without ever recording a win). Drongos are people who drag down the average level of performance. They may display one or more unhelpful traits – selfish, dishonest, poor timekeeper, lazy, dull or simply lacking a positive attitude to doing business. They are fairly easy to spot. We find them in shops where there is an uneasy atmosphere and a poor turn-over performance, and they are often resented by their work colleagues.

Most people in an organisation know who the drongos are, but it often takes a long time for the boss (who also knows) to face up to doing something about it. It is easy to find reasons to keep a poor performer on the payroll – 'He might get better', 'We can't find anyone to replace her', or 'The HR director won't let us do it without following a long-winded process that takes over three months'. All these considerations can cause a series of sleepless nights, but nothing changes the fact that your initial instinct was right. You will only be saved more anguish when the deed is done and the drongo has moved on to work for someone else.

Big companies tend to be the biggest wimps when it comes to firing people for poor performance. Organisations that are ruled by process often hand their human resources team total control of every decision about people. This can lead to a filing cabinet full of written warnings without a single case reaching its conclusion.

For managers at Timpson there is no reason to delay tackling the poor performers. Every area of the country is expected to have a waiting list of possible recruits who have already been inter-viewed, so we can always find someone keen to replace a colleague who leaves us. If possible we don't issue warning letters or put the colleague on a performance management programme that is, in truth, a device to build up a strong case ahead of a possible tribunal rather than an honest attempt to improve the colleague's performance. Instead we arrange a face-to-face meeting.

We have a simple message to the colleague who fails to match our standards: 'Your best will never be good enough for us, so it is time for you to find your happiness elsewhere.' We have this conversation as quickly as we can, because the sooner we part company the better it is for the business. But it is important to remember that we made a mistake by employing the wrong person, that is why we should be generous in our severance pay and employment advice. We genuinely wish to part as friends in the hope that our ex-colleague will find a more suitable job.

If our conversation fails and the drongo is unable to agree with our suggestion, the parting will still take place but it will take longer and be less friendly. That is when we start operating like the majority of employers by issuing warning letters and making the colleague stick rigidly to our contract of employment.

As soon as a drongo leaves, the business feels better. Colleagues no longer have to work alongside someone they didn't respect, managers have more time available to look after their superstars and I will guarantee the company will be more profitable. We have seen several cases when sales shoot up after cutting a store team from three down to two by losing a passenger.

Of course I hope that our ex-colleagues truly do find their happiness elsewhere, but saying goodbye to the drongos is essential if you want a business full of 9s and 10s.

Promote from within

———— ✤ ————

Never underrate your current colleagues –
they know much more about your business
than people coming from outside.

Strong businesses usually
rely on home-grown talent.

In 1997 our global competitor Mister Minit was sold by its owner, the Switzerland-based American, Don Hillsdon Ryan, to UBS, the Swiss bank. Mister Minit repaired shoes and cut keys in about fifteen countries through a total of nearly 3,000 shops. 500 were in the UK – my biggest competitor, but not particularly profitable. I went to see the UBS man in charge, Ian Siddall, with an offer to buy the UK business, but got a terse reply. 'We are experts', he told me, 'at buying family businesses and putting in professional management – and you are the next on our list!'

His professional idea was to turn Mister Minit into a multi-service business under a new brand – Minit Solutions. He decided to develop the model in the UK before spreading his new formula worldwide. He bought Sketchley to bring in dry cleaning and photo processing (Sketchley owned Supasnaps) and, with the help of market research and design consultants, set about building his new retail concept. As well as changing the shops he also changed the people. As each unit was refitted, the cobblers were demoted and branch management given to newly recruited graduates who couldn't cut a key. As a result wage costs doubled while turnover dropped dramatically. UBS made matters worse by reorganising the area team. Existing district managers, with only two O Levels (or GCSEs) but over twenty years' experience of the shoe repair trade, were ousted in favour of more academically qualified executives from elsewhere. It was tough for the new recruits, whose experience of area management in fashion, food retailing and travel agencies did nothing to equip them for the world of cobbling. Ian Siddall discovered his professional approach was a disaster, the UK shops recording a cumulative loss of £120m in only four years.

We learnt from their mistakes, and Timpson now take the opposite approach. Everyone joins us as a trainee manager and many have gone all the way to area and even regional management. We have over 30 area managers and more than 200 other colleagues helping to run the areas. They all started work for Timpson as an apprentice. We never consider employing a field executive from outside our company. Some people tell me that we risk becoming inward-looking, lacking in new ideas and ignoring the inspiration that can be injected by an outsider. I disagree. By picking people with the right personality, keen extroverts who like new projects, I'm happy to stay insular and avoid the risks you take by giving key jobs to outsiders.

At times impatient stockholders, facing a falling share price, insist on a change of chief executive. This almost always leads to writing off the cost of past sins and a profit warning, which is often greeted by an increase in the share price as the market anticipates the magic about to be created by their new leader. It doesn't always work – look at what happened at Iceland under Bill Grimsey and the lacklustre results as Marks & Spencer handed the baton from one new leader to another.

Of course some outside appointments are fantastically successful. Isaac Wolfson saved Great Universal Stores from going bust and then made it into one of the most successful companies of the last 75 years. Woolworths might be synonymous with failure now, but in the 1990s Geoff Mulcahy came from outside to turn a lame-duck Woolworths into a flourishing group called Kingfisher.

In many areas, away from business, external appointments appear to be the norm. Teachers usually flit from school to school to rise up the pay scale and the same migration occurs in the civil service. It can't be good for morale when your best talent has to look elsewhere to get promotion.

I am particularly bewildered by my favourite football club, Manchester City, who spent over £500m building a fabulous training academy and yet still pay over £100m a season to import new players from elsewhere. I know there is always pressure to buy a world-class superstar but we seldom see a home-grown player on the Etihad pitch (most Academy graduates are transferred to another club).

I also have been guilty of putting my faith in superstars appointed from elsewhere. In 1985 when Timpson shoe shops were hitting the wall I chickened out by kicking myself upstairs to be Chairman and brought in a team from the Burton Group, the premier retail team of the day. On reflection they had no chance – we were facing fierce competition and their expertise was in clothes not shoes. The Timpson old-timers with all the inside knowledge watched in despair; their wisdom wasn't wanted by a new team intent on putting their faith in modern retailing. To solve the problem I sold the shoe shops and even today still feel both guilty and disappointed. In those days we never thought much about succession planning.

Despite our company's commitment to promote from within, we still have the occasional lapse. It is so tempting to think the rest of the world must be right and follow their example by going into the recruitment market hoping to find a new superstar with a magic wand.

These appointments often seem to start so well, with the organisation giving the new star a warm welcome and anticipating success well before the newcomer has produced any results. Very quickly you may discover more newcomers than you expected. The new boss often brings their old PA and may poach key players from their last organisation at salaries substantially higher than you are used to paying. You will also redecorate their offices and add to the company fleet of cars. Sometimes they perform the promised miracle but on many occasions anticipation turns to disappointment followed by the expensive job of saying goodbye. It usually takes two years to recognise that you made the wrong choice.

You won't always make the right internal appointment. Some of our area managers find it difficult to cope with the extra responsibility. We are usually able to save the situation by giving them their old job back. It isn't so easy to handle an external appointment that doesn't work out.

When you think you've finally learnt your lesson it is easy to repeat the mistake. In 2005, when we decided to develop a locksmith business, we recruited qualified locksmiths and, if they couldn't cope, gave the surplus work to expert sub-contractors. We struggled to provide a quality service and the business barely made any money. Eventually we found the answer by recruiting some of our successful cobblers who were keen to go out on the road. They went on an intensive internal locksmith course and immediately made a difference. Today, the majority of our 50 mobile locksmiths have come out of our shops and the locksmith subsidiary is heading towards profits of £1m a year.

Internal appointments not only save the cost of a recruitment consultant, they also come with a greater degree of certainty – you know who you are getting and they understand your culture. Harry Levison of British Shoe Corporation built one of the most talented buying teams in retail history by plucking potential buyers from around the business. The two architects of Tesco's retail domination, Ian MacLaurin and Terry Leahy, both started off stacking shelves.

It took at least ten years for us to establish our company culture and we find it takes new recruits at least three years before it becomes part of their personality. Every time you take on a new boss from outside, you put the culture in jeopardy.

Sometimes external appointments are inevitable, especially for specialists in areas like accountancy and IT. But don't despair – although imported managers come with a high level of risk, there are plenty of exceptions like Paresh, our Finance Director, who joined us eleven years ago, totally got our culture within a year and for the last decade has played a big part in making it even better.

Be wary of outsiders

———— ✕ ————

*Plenty of people think they know
how to improve your business.*

**Ensure newcomers understand
your culture before they
tell you what to do.**

Every day several emails tell me how we can 'improve our bottom line'. Some say how much better things will be if we use their footfall tracker analysis, others can make things better by studying the social/economic mix in our catchment area. I am told constantly to embrace the world of 'Big Data' to drive a better customer experience.

New pieces of legislation bring invitations to breakfast meetings held by lawyers, accountants, actuaries and bankers all keen to explain, over a few complimentary croissants, how they can, at the normal hourly rate, make sure you comply with new Health and Safety regulations, take full advantage of the apprentice levy rules and introduce their latest idea on salary sacrifices.

We have decided never to appoint another outsider to any senior general management role. We can't train our own IT specialists and we occasionally have to look outside for accountants but every apprentice is regarded as a trainee manager. We are able to fill all our field management vacancies through internal appointments, so never face the turmoil that can be created when a new broom sweeps into a top role. You not only get a new face, with values that will undoubtedly differ from your own company culture, but they often surround themselves with their own team and like to be advised by pet consultants. A change at the top is certain to change the culture. For us, protecting the culture is such a high priority that we won't take the risk of appointing top managers from elsewhere.

Despite this homespun prejudice, we get great support from a whole range of advisors. We all need accountants to sign off the books and provide technical advice – the tax system is so complicated that the advice of a clever tax expert is essential. But avoid any of the innovative tax planning schemes that, I have discovered through bitter experience, can cost you much more than you save in tax, while still providing fees to the accountant. These days if a tax planning scheme doesn't feel right, the taxman will make sure it doesn't work and make you pay for the inconvenience.

Every business needs a lawyer and I am eternally grateful to Roger Lane-Smith who masterminded our management buyout and many of our other deals. But lawyers sometimes seem to forget who they are working for. I'm not campaigning for a lawyer-free society – we need a legal profession to keep control of the rules – but there is a danger that once lawyers get involved they think it is their deal not yours. It can become a sport, with one lawyer playing against the solicitor acting for the other side. The game uses an armoury of warranties and indemnities, stored on computer from previous encounters. The aim is to score points by smuggling through a few devious new clauses hidden among many pages of old favourites.

For reasons I still don't understand, competitive lawyers often fight the final stages of their battle in the middle of the night, raising niggling deal-breakers when they hope the opposition is too tired to argue. While some lawyers are piling up the warranties, others are developing a growing list of contract clauses that are often found in the small print. This practice now means that before completing any contract you need a lawyer to tell you what you are signing up for.

It isn't surprising that the legal fees charged to settle difficult disputes can be far greater than the settlement itself. Obstinate lawyers, by persuading their clients to dig in for a better deal, can keep the fees coming in for so long that this endless fee-earner is described by at least one lawyer as 'the dripping roast'.

Some may be surprised to know that one of my all-time star advisers was a bank manager, Brian Ferguson from NatWest, who put his reputation on the line to secure the extra £500k we needed to complete the purchase of Automagic in September 1995. Brian should never have been put in that precarious position, but NatWest, even then, was riddled with rules and our lending had to be approved by people in London who never met me and knew nothing about our business. Brian did know, which is why he gave us his backing. He acted like a proper old-fashioned bank manager who was trusted with a bit of Upside Down Management. Today, the best way to deal with banks is to be the one who is lending them the money. Sadly the banking sector is one of the prime examples of process being put before people.

I have had plenty more good advisers, but few to match the two who have helped me for many years and thoroughly understood the Timpson culture. Michael McAvoy advised me on corporate communications, not really advertising or PR but the art of seeing things from the other person's point of view. It was a valuable lesson and for over 40 years Michael was at the end of the phone ready and willing to act as one of my mentors. He made me think and made sure that I created our sort of culture in my way while he helpfully watched it happen.

The other star is Jools Payne, who writes, edits and puts the energy into our weekly newsletter *Timpson Weekly News* (TWN), which is the subject of another chapter. I was very happy to hand over total editorial responsibility to Jools because I knew that she fully understood our culture, loved the business and loved talking to our colleagues. Her enthusiasm shines through week after week. TWN plays a very important part in communicating our culture and I wouldn't want to give the editorial job to anyone else.

So I have some positive tales to tell about bringing outsiders into the business, but I still advise anyone to be wary of strangers who promise to work miracles for a business they know little about. I learnt a lesson when I brought in a design consultant to refresh the look of our shops in 1994. They spent six weeks looking at our shops and asking me loads of questions about the business before coming back with their big idea – use a different colour to promote each of our services. Unimpressed, I went to Bath, which has always been a city with some character, took a photo of every shop fascia I liked, pinned all the pictures up on a wall in our office and picked the one I liked best. That is still the colour and type style we use today.

I cringe in disbelief whenever I remember a project named KeyCall, which was an attempt to provide a roadside rescue service for motorists stranded without a key. We solved a lot of the technical problems, found a friendly call centre and enough good, willing couriers to get cut keys anywhere in the country within a couple of hours, but half our development cost was spent on marketing and market research. I was persuaded by a consultant to carry out an in-depth survey of two small but cleverly targeted groups of 24 people at a time, that revealed we were on a winner. To get customers signing up, they recommended putting flyers, for a month, in the weekend national papers. I started to have my doubts on the first weekend when, outside my local Delamere Stores, I saw a man standing over the rubbish bin outside the shop, shaking all the loose advertising material out of his papers before he drove home. It cost us nearly £100k to develop and launch the scheme and we only ever signed up ten customers, including a girl in the office who was testing the call centre and one of my aunts who was just trying to do me a favour.

Some businesses forget that professional advisors are suppliers and it is totally reasonable, as a customer, to negotiate a fee and expect value for money. Too often the biggest surprise during a deal is when your lawyer or accountant presents their final fee. Don't be shy, be prepared to question the figure and if possible set some guidelines from the very start. Even if you keep a close eye on professional fees, deals are always expensive, but we are never tempted to add to the cost by getting a merchant bank to do the deal on our behalf. It's our money, our business and we don't want anyone else negotiating our deal.

A new, expensive and dangerous practice is creeping into many parts of the business world: the need to seek independent, professional advice. It is popular with pension trustees and non-executive directors who are keen to cover their backs while delivering their governance. Professional advisors are getting extra income because experience, intuition and inspired risk-taking are no longer trusted. By being safe and sticking to best practice and a proper process, companies are paying more fees and losing the edge that comes from entrepreneurial flair.

I fear that government will want to increase the regulation of business and provide even more reasons for the professional advisors to invite us all to a breakfast seminar. But what we really need is some Upside Down Government. Rather than bringing out more laws telling businesspeople how to run a business, civil servants should realise that their role is to provide us with the support we need and trust us with the freedom to do our job.

The decision to leave the EU gives our government the chance to do just that.

Look after the superstars

*Once you have found a few superstars,
make sure that you love them to bits.*

**Always find time to look after
your star performers.**

I was brought up in a family business that looked after its employees. I watched my father sign over 1,000 Christmas cards every year, sending a personal message to every shop and individual members of the management team. He was proud of the final salary company pension scheme which was allocated a significant slice of each year's profits, and I spent many very full days with him visiting our shops and chatting to as many members of staff as possible. Before 1975, when I became Managing Director, I wasn't qualified to attend the annual long-service lunch when the company recognised those employees who had been with the business for 25 or 45 years. I have since hosted 40 years of long-service lunches that now take place at my Cheshire home, a relaxed day when loyal colleagues, accompanied by their partners, are my guests for lunch and a leisurely stroll round the garden.

Lots of other businesses do the same, although many colleagues find well-established benefits disappear if their company is acquired by another group. Our employee benefit package has survived a series of corporate restructurings and we honour the past service record of new colleagues who join us through an acquisition. In 2003 when we celebrated 100 years of shoe repairing I gave every colleague their birthday off, a perk so popular it has been retained ever since. Others thought we were being too generous – some accountants asked me how much the scheme cost and were surprised when I claimed that giving people an extra paid holiday on their birthday actually made us money. It became part of our culture, a guarantee that all colleagues matter at Timpson, and I have no doubt the reduction in days off sick was a direct result of the birthdays off and our relaxed attitude to colleagues needing time off for genuine reasons such as dental appointments and emergency childcare.

The success of the birthdays off encouraged us to look for more ways to amaze our colleagues. We now send a certificate and a letter signed by me to every colleague who completes one year's service, and they get another two years later. The certificates I send for five years and every five years after that are accompanied by a tax-free cheque. Special birthdays – 21st, 30th, 40th, etc. – bring a bottle of champagne. We also like to celebrate marriages by providing the wedding car driven by Martin (who drives myself or my son James during the week) and giving the colleague who got married an extra week's paid holiday for the honeymoon.

One big lesson I have learnt is that when a star performer goes off the boil and falls short of past results, the reason is often nothing to do with work. A variety of life's challenges can get in the way – drugs, relationship problems, debt, bereavement, gambling, alcohol, or simply an attack of stress or depression can lie behind a sudden change in demeanour and consequent loss of the enthusiasm that had previously created success. It is our job, if possible, to help. A loan, bereavement leave, referral to the right medical support, or just the chance to unload big problems onto a sympathetic boss can change their home life and put the colleague's day-to-day performance back on track.

It's a big mistake to think that you can set up a superb reward system by writing a set of rules and regulations. We don't have a wage structure – everyone's pay is reviewed on the anniversary date that they joined the company. That way we make sure that we reward the talents of the individual. We have a guideline, so most colleagues get the recommended increase, but superstars can have their outstanding performance fully recognised.

I recommend carrying out a totally politically incorrect exercise. We already keep a check on our drongos (we usually put them under the heading 'colleagues of concern'). If they stay on that list for more than three months we would expect them to be asked to find their happiness elsewhere. There is no doubt that by keeping the company clear from poor performers you are helping to look after the top colleagues, who don't want to work shoulder to shoulder with people who don't get the culture and don't pull their weight. You need to keep a second list, a roll call of your superstars. Look at that second list every month and ask yourself the question: 'When did you last do something special to thank this gem in your business?'

I totally believe in our particular form of discrimination. I would never condone discrimination based on gender or race, and I'm keen push up the bar on employing physically and mentally disabled people, but I will always discriminate in favour of those that bring a positive attitude to work and breed success, and against the minority of selfish, jobsworth under-performers who don't 'get it'.

Don't be tempted to save money by paying people less than they deserve. Look at the net pay of those colleagues whom you rate 9 or 10 out of 10 and consult your conscience. Are you happy that they are properly rewarded for their excellence? If not, do something about it. Never mind what the company pay policy may say – paying great people over the odds always pays off.

I must make it absolutely clear that rewards systems should never be governed by a process. Fair enough, everyone gets their birthday off and a cheque whenever they reach each year-of-service landmark, but any praise that is designed to recognise excellence is much better if it is an impromptu gesture tailored to celebrate a magic moment. There is no greater 'wow' factor than a reward that comes with a big element of surprise.

The perks we and our colleagues value most are those that only go to special people. Drongos and poor performers aren't given a chance to use our free-stay holiday homes and it takes an exceptional act to be singled out for one of my Chairman's Awards – a handwritten letter attached to a tax-paid cheque for £100 or more.

One of the most popular of these merit-based perks is our scheme that makes dreams come true. We ask colleagues to let us know what they would wish to happen in their wildest dreams and we promise to make at least one colleague's dream come true every month. It costs us less than £100,000 a year and is money massively well spent. We have funded some fantastic family reunions with long-lost relatives on the other side of the world. We have paid for weddings, one divorce, dental treatment, a house extension and even the purchase of a rare breed of dog, all dream projects for successful colleagues. Area teams have wine and chocolates in the boot of their car ready to hand out as a mark of success. They also have a pocket full of our special scratch cards (not the lottery type but a Timpson version). Winning colleagues scratch the card to discover the reward, which can range from £10 to £50 plus a bottle of their choice, a meal out on James and, the big gamble, the next sale through the till is yours!

It is so much easier to give appropriate praise to your top performers if you really know your people, particularly if you know what makes them tick outside work. That is why we regularly check our managers' knowledge with a 'know your people' test. We ask them a number of questions about one of the colleagues in their team – names of their children, football team, favourite holiday destination and taste in music. We have already contacted the colleague in question to check the right answers. The quiz makes an important point: a good boss knows an awful lot about the members of their team.

One of our most important benefits is the hardship fund. Many of our colleagues, despite being great at repairing shoes and cutting keys, manage to make a bit of a mess of their personal budgeting. As long as the debt hasn't reached bankruptcy proportions we are always keen to help by lending the sum needed to bridge the gap. We have been lending money this way for over twenty years, so we have plenty of experience to prove that these loans get the colleague's mind back on the job, it avoids the temptation to pinch cash from the till and resolves a lot of the tension that existed at home.

Every week we celebrate individual success in our newsletter and perhaps, one day, I will copy Pret A Manger by having pictures of our all-time service champions on the wall of the staircase at the office.

We will never stop finding new ways to praise our superstars. If a customer writes to me complimenting the service in their local shop (and I'm pleased to say plenty do), I write a handwritten letter of thanks and send a framed copy of the customer's correspondence to be displayed in the shop. In recent years I have included pictures of our unsung heroes on the back page of our annual report and at a party to celebrate my 70th birthday I presented prizes to my lifetime legends.

Praise plays a big part in Upside Down Management – every boss has the authority to pick the perfect way to congratulate members of their team. There are no rules and no budget; the best praise is spontaneous, so our managers have the authority to spend whatever it takes whenever they want to make a star performer feel extra special.

12

Rescue over-promoted colleagues

Don't fire colleagues just because you promoted them too far.

Never be tempted to let employment lawyers organise a round of redundancy.

This fairly short but important chapter strikes at the heart of your company culture. I have already talked about making sure that you say goodbye to drongos and that your business is full of colleagues who rate 9 and 10 out of 10, but that doesn't mean you should sack people over 50 who find it tough to keep up with the pace of change, or anyone who you have promoted beyond their ability.

If you throw out loyal and long-serving colleagues just because they appear to have gone beyond their sell-by date you will do serious damage to the company's credibility. It happens far too often when companies embark on a cost-cutting programme and require everyone to reapply for their own jobs, or declare that a department is subject to a round of redundancies.

If you have to reduce the workforce, listen to your conscience rather than the employment lawyers. I am still embarrassed that I stood by in 2004 while we told everyone in our finance department that they were at risk of redundancy. We were following legal advice but it was a lie. We sent the threatening letter to several long-serving superstars who were never facing the slightest risk. We gave them a series of sleepless nights and lost respect just to satisfy a pedantic process.

If you have a policy, which we do, of promoting from within the company, you should do everything possible to help long-serving colleagues stay on the payroll until their retirement, but that doesn't mean they must stay in the same job. Our area managers, who fulfil a vital role, will do well to stay in the role for over fifteen years – it is a young person's job with long hours and loads of stress.

As a stress sufferer myself I am extremely sympathetic. I know what it's like living your life looking at the rest of the world wishing you could feel as capable as they look. When stress arrives you wake every morning hoping that you have returned to your old relaxed self, only to find that you are facing another day switching between misery and butterflies in your stomach. There is never any calm, every moment is spent turning trivial problems over in your mind, unable to make even the easiest decision.

Some area managers have the constitution of an ox and can cope for decades, but most need a change of career before retirement. Others, like managers in other parts of the business, have been promoted a step too far, and some simply find it difficult to keep up with the new challenges of a fast-moving business.

If a new recruit fails to match expectations they should be asked to leave as nicely, as quickly and as generously as possible, but the same does not apply to long-serving and loyal colleagues. Don't leave them where they are, but find a role that gives them job satisfaction and a chance to make a positive contribution to the company.

Remember, they are the same people who played a big role in the past and you should know the strengths they can bring to the future, but be honest, tell them the truth and don't invent a non-job that keeps them on the payroll but cuts them out of the day-to-day business. And be blunt: if it means taking on less responsibility, the salary and perks should reflect the new job, but give them a one-off payment to compensate.

We currently have 28 ex-area managers who have moved on to new roles. Some have become Regional Managers, and one is Gouy, our Colleague Support Director, but most have returned to branch management. By understanding the situation and taking an adult approach, the colleague is happier at work and the company can benefit from a wealth of experience.

Every month I send out letters to colleagues who have completed 25, 30, 35 and even 40 years' service. Many are still with us because we have the flexibility to find the job that suits them best at each stage of their career. Their contribution is very important to me and strengthens our business.

Create a great company culture

---✕---

Your company culture will follow your beliefs,
especially if you believe in your people.

In a dynamic company everything
fits together, every colleague sees
the world through the same pair
of eyes, but the Chief Executive
is the visionary who not only
'gets it' but also gets how to
get everyone else to 'get it'.

In 2006 my son James, who was firmly established as our Chief Executive, went on a fact-finding tour to the United States alongside 25 other upwardly mobile senior managers. He visited Southwest Airlines, WL Gore, MGM and Ritz Carlton. I was worried that James would come back with enough radical ideas to signal the end of my involvement with the Timpson strategy.

My fears were unfounded. James returned full of new ideas but with no hint of a U-turn. 'We do most of the things they do already', he said. 'They have the same values and follow the same principles, but they are much better at talking about it. All the businesses I saw know what has made them great, they understand the big factor that binds their business together and continues to create their success. In short, they all have a clear company culture which they never stop talking about. We also have loads of ideas that work, but it is time to tell everyone what they are. We have a company culture just like all the fabulous businesses you paid a lot of money for me to visit, but it is now time to talk about the Timpson culture.'

So, instead of making me redundant, James gave me two new jobs. First he asked me to write a book about what he called 'The Magic Dust', a catalogue of the things we do that have created our success. To discover what to put in the book I went on a company-wide tour to talk to colleagues from every part of the business. I wanted to know how they viewed the company so I could understand our company culture through the eyes of our colleagues.

I learnt a lot, not just about our business, but also about our people, why they work for us and the things we do that matter most. It wasn't long before I was able to recognise the components of our 'magic dust', and I realised why it was so important to tell the world of Timpson all about them, because the things that mattered most were things that other businesses didn't do. The book talked about Upside Down Management, birthdays off, our holiday homes and the importance of picking people for their personality. I gave it a strange title, *How to Ride a Giraffe*, because someone once said our business is like a giraffe – no one would have designed it but it seems to work really well.

Writing the book helped me understand the various components that make up the Timpson culture, but, being realistic, only a small percentage of our colleagues would read it, so James gave me my second new job when he asked me to devise a new management course for our senior team. We called it our Leadership Course and quickly decided that the only way to tell everyone about our culture was for James and myself to run the course ourselves.

It took a big bite out of our diaries. We not only delivered every part of each two-day course ourselves but also hosted a dinner for every course. It made such a difference getting the message from the Chairman and the Chief Executive that we are still running leadership courses ten years later. I can't think of a better way for the boss to create the company culture.

Our Leadership Course is all about people – how you pick them, how you support them and why some must be asked to leave. It is people who create a company's culture. Our culture has been helped by recruiting like-minded personalities who have the same values. It is strengthened by our involvement with children's charities and by employing ex-offenders, but little things can also be very important. When we took over the management of Morrisons' dry cleaning business it made a big impression when our area managers bought a kettle and some tea bags for every branch team. They immediately realised they had joined a company that cares about people.

Seven years ago we recognised that our culture is so important, we should establish a culture committee to discuss how we can do more for our colleagues through our hardship fund, better training, more social events, and by helping colleagues when they encounter personal problems. Five years ago we started telling customers about our culture using the graphics in Timpson shops. It has certainly done no harm to replace the posters that advertised our latest key cutting deal with one telling our customers that all our colleagues get their birthday off. Many of our customers like to feel part of the Timpson culture.

You will perhaps have noticed that I haven't attempted to define precisely what I mean by culture. A strong culture can't be created by putting in a process, there aren't any rules, it can't be dreamt up by issuing a mission statement and it certainly won't be established by bringing in a team of consultants. It is a vague, intangible concept that is crystal clear to colleagues who 'get it'. It is the glue that binds the organisation together by uniting like-minded people in a common purpose. A company with a strong and positive culture will be consistent in treating colleagues, customers and suppliers with honesty and respect, and they, in turn, will be proud to be associated with the company values. Most partners in the John Lewis Partnership have a clear idea what their company stands for, but the same wasn't true in BHS, for example.

Company cultures come in all shapes and sizes. Most are positive but some can be distinctly negative, and they are nearly all strongly influenced by the Chief Executive, whose personality is inevitably stamped on the whole enterprise. But, however good

CEOs may be, they can't create a worthwhile culture if they build their career by flitting from one job to a better paid role every three years. It takes years to establish a strong culture. You can't change attitudes with one memo and you won't create a culture change during a Board meeting.

Culture is a difficult concept to tie down; it's different for each company and it defines the organisation's personality. If you are lucky enough to have created a positive culture it will be the most valuable intangible asset on your balance sheet, so invest a lot of your time trying to make sure it gets even stronger.

14

No Head Office

Don't let people who seldom go near a shop tell front-line troops what to do.

We banned answering machines – the nearest person picks up the phone and does what they can to help.

When I started work in 1960 every ordinary worker clocked in and out of the office, but management had special dining rooms and used segregated lavatories. Most people smoked at their desk and women's wages were about two-thirds of the rate for men.

I remember the room full of girls wearing our regulation blue uniform dress sitting in rows calculating our stock and sales figures on adding machines (it was two years before we introduced our first computer – it filled a room nearly as big as a tennis court and took all night to tackle a calculation that my iPad would spit out in milliseconds).

If you had a car it had to be parked at the back of the warehouse, a good 400 yards from the main entrance, but there were 40 parking places in the prime spot – number 1 was opposite the door while number 40 was 100 yards away. The parking bay was a clear indication of your place in the corporate pecking order. No women were senior enough to qualify for a parking spot, nor did they get to eat in the top two dining rooms (directors' and senior executives') and only Doris Ferguson, our welfare officer, qualified to enter the junior executives' dining area. It was almost impossible for women to secure promotion, there was no maternity leave and most pregnant workers left with their P45. All the senior executives' lavatories were men only, as no one ever imagined a woman taking on a big management role. But everyone knew that one woman wielded a lot of power – Teresa Dutton, who was secretary to my grandfather and then my father before helping me negotiate my first three years as Managing Director.

It was a very different world in which Head Office was where it all happened. Good performers in our shops were rewarded with promotion to Head Office, which ran the business through a strict set of rules – the *Standing Orders for Shoe Repair Factories*. Area managers acted as policemen out in the field with little freedom to use their initiative. They weren't even allowed to pick their own branch managers – every appointment had to be approved by Billy MacKenzie, the director who ran the staff office.

All new appointments had to be confirmed in person, which meant that managers came to Head Office for a face-to-face meeting that usually lasted little more than ten minutes. One left home in Nottingham at 5.30 in the morning to arrive at the office before 9.00am, but unfortunately he parked in bay 2, which was allocated to deputy chairman Geoffrey Noakes. Geoffrey was so irritated he blocked in the innocent manager, who was forced to wait in the reception area until Geoffrey left for home at 5.45pm.

Although we now have equal pay and have broken down much of the divide that existed between levels of management, the idea of a business being run by the people based in Head Office is a stereotype that still exists in most businesses today. I'm often asked 'Where do you run the business from?', 'How many people do you have in Head Office?' and 'How often do you go to the office?', as if the office is the only place where the important work is done. Ever since we introduced Upside Down Management I have made it crystal clear that we don't have a head office. Everyone who isn't in a branch is paid to support the people who repair shoes, take passport photos and give great service to our customers. I don't want people who seldom go near a shop telling our front-line troops how to do their job.

By 1995 we lived in a very different world to the workplace

I saw in the 1960s. We had equal pay, women in senior manage-ment, one canteen and no designated parking bays. But it was still referred to as Head Office, housing colleagues who issued orders to shop teams who saw every memo or phone call from Timpson House as an instruction.

My new way of management meant attitudes had to change. It took five years before the message really got across and the team at Timpson House understood that they were there to support their shop colleagues, not to tell them what to do. We banned memos and insisted everyone spent a day working in a shop each year. The reception area of the office was redesigned to look like a shop as a daily reminder of the business that makes our money. The knowledge that it takes the profits of one of our aver-age shops to pay the employment costs of an extra office worker made us look hard at what everyone did at Timpson House and cut out roles that made no contribution to our bottom line.

It was a big culture change and we met plenty of resentment. Suddenly the role of Head Office had shifted and colleagues in the field became the most important people in the business. To encourage the Timpson office team to see their new support function as a positive role, we encouraged them with praise and loved them to bits. We started by putting £1,000 behind the bar of a local pub on the last Friday of every month and introduced a number of new perks including free football tickets (we have three company season tickets at Manchester City), free breakfast and a series of social events and leisure trips.

Eventually most people 'got it' (though a few had to move on), but the atmosphere completely changed when the office got a dramatic makeover including wacky wallpaper, big open spaces, a fireman's pole, a vastly improved Cobblers' Cafe, a gym and a tennis court. We were showing our support colleagues that they didn't need to issue orders to make a massive influence on the service we give our customers.

We moved into Timpson House in 1987, and just about everything has changed except the car park. We have over ten times as many shops but still have the same number of parking places. One is reserved for the colleague of the month, but for everyone else, if you arrive after 8.30am you will probably have to park by the warehouse 300 yards down the road, which is where my car was yesterday.

Everyone knows the boss

———❈———

It's great if you know everyone by name, but what really matters is that every colleague knows who you are.

Cut across the management structure and talk to everyone.

I will never forget the day that one of the Timpson directors came to the shop in Altrincham where I had just started work as the most junior trainee. He spoke to Bill Branston, the manager, and Jessie McLeod, who ran the ladies' and children's shoe department, but he didn't even smile at me. I felt a very small cog in a very big wheel. That experience taught me an important lesson: whenever I visit one of our shops I try to have a word with every colleague.

As soon as I became a shoe buyer I followed the example set by my father and grandfather and called at as many shops as possible, usually carrying a bag full of samples, so the colleagues could see and comment on the styles I was contemplating buying for the following season. It was still in the days when they all called me Mr John but they quickly discovered that I wasn't always stuck behind a desk.

I don't believe anyone can be an invisible leader. Every business is bound to become an extension of the Chief Executive's personality. The person who sets the strategy also determines and communicates the culture. If all the colleagues know and respect the CEO it is so much easier to get the message across. Memos, policy statements, company announcements and even a picture of the CEO with a personal message all mean a lot more if the recipients feel they know the character behind the communication.

Once, unusually for me, I struck up a conversation with a perfect stranger who was sitting opposite me on a train, not long after it had left Euston. I soon discovered he was a regular customer at our branch in Bank Underground station. He was surprised that I knew the shop and amazed that I could tell him the name of the branch manager at the time, Martin Winter. Some colleagues stand out from the crowd and you are bound to remember their name, but I still struggle if I meet one of them out of context, particularly in a departure lounge when they are going off on holiday. I am careful never to claim that I know the majority of our colleagues ever since I did a live interview one Sunday night for BBC Radio 5. I was on my own, in a Manchester studio, talking to a presenter miles away who said, 'You're famous for knowing the names of all your employees'. Although I've never made that claim, I started to panic. 'Can you tell me', he continued, 'the name of your manager in High Street Birmingham?' With relief I was able to reply: 'We don't have a shop in High Street Birmingham.'

Shortly after we bought the Morrisons dry cleaning business I was just leaving their store in Speke when the guy behind the tobacco counter called me over. 'Did I hear it right? Are you Mr Timpson?' Once I had owned up to my identity he went on: 'First time I've ever seen a boss from the office.'

If you ask most shop assistants who they work for and who is their boss they will talk about the branch manager or the regional controller. Few will mention the Chief Executive, because many won't know who he or she is. Newly appointed CEOs often make a great start by spending the first few weeks out of the office and meeting lots of colleagues, but too many think that one trip round the business is enough. Good CEOs never stop visiting the business.

Becoming a well-known personality throughout the company shouldn't be thought of as an ego trip – it is an important part of building trust and creating the company culture. Every week I am reminded just how important, whenever I am told: 'At last I've got to meet you.' When I recently visited a pod outside the Tesco in Ferndown I was greeted by a colleague who I had never met before. 'I've been with the company for six months, read two of your books and heard you on *Desert Island Discs* but I never thought I would see you in Ferndown.'

Today's confirmation that your profile has hit the spot is when you are asked, 'Can I have a selfie?' Once recognised, all you need to do is to use your profile to help your colleagues and improve the business.

Keep walking round
the business

Statistics provide only part of the picture.
Fill in the gaps by getting out of the office.

In a world full of social media
the best form of communication
is still meeting face-to-face.

In the last year I have visited over 800 of our outlets, travelling 35,000 miles. Why would a 73 year-old man want to spend an average of two days a week going round shops?

We make our money by repairing shoes, cutting keys, taking passport photos and providing many more services. None of these jobs happen in the office. If you want to see what we do, meet a customer or talk to the colleagues who bring in our business, you have to visit our shops. Our management accounts measure the company's performance, but the figures only come to life when you escape from your office and tour round the business. Many respected and successful business leaders have said that you can't do good business simply by sitting behind your desk, but far too few executives think trips round the company are more important than sitting in a meeting.

In a lot of big organisations, shop-floor colleagues know nothing about the person who runs the business – they probably don't even know their name. It makes a massive difference if the leader spreads his or her character throughout the organisation and the best way to communicate is to meet colleagues face-to-face. Taking the trouble to travel round the business, and chat to all the colleagues you meet, has a positive impact that can't be matched by memos, newsletters, blogs or video links.

I like the way one boss walks round his office every day starting with five coins in his left pocket. Every time he is able to praise a colleague or give them a compliment he moves a coin from left to right and he keeps walking and talking until his left-hand pocket is empty.

The conversation doesn't have to be about business. When I meet a colleague in their branch I don't just want to talk shop, I also want them to tell me about themselves. Consequently

I've heard some amazing stories of the jobs they did before they joined us and the hobbies they pursue in their spare time (I have met an international croquet player, a professional boxer, a seriously hairy biker and lots of people who play regular gigs for a band). Inevitably I hear about their children, their football team, their last round of golf and most recent holiday.

I try to talk to everybody. I probably won't go to the shop again for another two years so it would be terrible to ignore anyone.

I don't have an agenda, and certainly don't tour our shops to catch people out. I want to see things from a customer's perspective and hope to spot some ideas that we can spread throughout the company. The development of both our watch repairing and mobile phone repair business was created using ideas produced by people working in our shops.

Although I'm not looking for trouble, it's wrong to walk past a problem, especially when a colleague is breaking one of our two rules ('Look the part' and 'Put the money in the till'). If I am really worried about standards in a shop or the attitude of a colleague I immediately telephone the area manager and ask: 'I've just been to "x branch" – what can you tell me about it?' Usually they are well aware of the problem and have a plan. If I find more poor shops in the same area I ring the Regional Manager to check whether the area team is in difficulty.

Sometimes I travel with a member of the sales team but normally I'm on my own. I don't give advanced warning, so the first visit of the day can come as a big surprise, but it doesn't take long for news to spread and I've often answered the telephone in a shop to be told 'John is on his way!' On the rare occasions I go out on a Sunday the colleagues are very surprised but appear pretty pleased to see me. It makes a difference when you take the trouble to meet people working unsocial hours.

Every so often someone seeks my advice. They ask 'Can I have a word?' and take me on one side, away from the shop floor. I'm never sure what will come next, it could be about fostering or stress, an issue with the area team or in one case a manager who made a massive blunder and wanted me to advise how to break the news to his area manager. On occasions the colleague turns out to be a whistleblower, keen to stir up trouble for his boss. It's a conversation that usually starts, 'No one will have the courage to tell you this, but …' Whatever the question or complaint I just listen. Sometimes there is a problem with the area management, on other occasions the problem lies with the person making the complaint. These exchanges provide an interesting part of the colour painted during a day walking round the business.

Managers who spend every day stuck behind a desk miss the most interesting and important part of the job.

Town Hall meetings

---❧---

*Everyone gets the same message
at the same time.*

**If you don't give a regular
update, someone will say,
'No one tells me anything'.**

There is a particular Town Hall meeting I will never forget. One day in April 1987, I gathered together everyone in our Wythenshawe warehouse and office to tell them that I had sold the Timpson shoe shops. Although it wasn't for me to say so, this almost certainly meant that the purchaser, multiple shoe shop competitor, George Oliver, would close down the site and make everyone redundant.

It was a tough task, made worse by the fact that I had spent a lot of the past year hidden in my office. It taught me the importance of keeping everyone up to date with the news, good and bad, by gathering everyone together on a regular basis, something we now call our Town Hall meetings.

I am often asked how we manage to communicate with our colleagues in the field, with so many shops spread across the country, but it is surprisingly easy to keep our far-flung colleagues up to date – it is more difficult with those closer to home. In our workshops, warehouses and office, where a lot of people are working together, there is more opportunity to spread a rumour and a greater opportunity to observe the comings and goings of senior executives, leading to speculation about the latest plot. We try to be as open as possible (all the meeting rooms have a glass front so everyone can see what is going on even if they can't hear), but still, occasionally, we get someone saying, 'No one tells me anything'.

It is important to make Town Hall meetings part of the routine – if colleagues are called to a meeting out of the blue, it is bound to cause speculation and most people will fear the worst. James, our Chief Executive, now has a 'Town Hall' every three to five weeks. They seldom take much longer than ten minutes, but that is enough time to welcome any new starters, mention anyone with a birthday, talk about the latest sales and profit figures, report on new shops, refits and acquisitions, highlight any imminent events in our social calendar and hand out a prize to the winner of our tidiest office competition.

It isn't just what you say that is important but also the way you say it. Be relaxed, tell nothing but the truth and say it with a smile. Your words might be designed to breed confidence but your body language has just as big an influence on whether you can communicate a confident feeling of optimism.

Sometimes, James calls a special meeting to make a particularly important announcement – when we have just bought another business, or sadly, on one occasion when one of our colleagues met a sudden and tragic death. As his Town Hall meetings are such a regular event, calling people together ahead of hearing such significant news doesn't cause any premature or unwelcome speculation.

In a world full of emails and Twitter it might seem old-fashioned to communicate by standing up in front of everybody. But our Town Hall meeting is the best way of making sure that everyone receives exactly the same message at the same time. Not everybody reads their emails and not every colleague follows James on Twitter. If a Prime Minister wants to spell out a message to the nation, a lectern is put in the middle of Downing Street and the whole nation can capture the words as they are spoken.

We have a weekly newsletter, an annual report, and a massive amount of Timpson news exchanged on social media, but nothing has taken the place of the old-fashioned Town Hall meeting.

You run PR

—❧—

*It makes a big difference when
journalists talk to the boss.*

**We don't have a marketing or
PR department but most people
have heard of Timpson.**

When, in 1975, I was appointed as Managing Director of Timpson, by Stuart Lyons, the UDS main Board director who became my Chairman, he wanted to make the most of the fact that we are a family business. Within weeks, with my wife Alex's permission, we put pictures of our three children, Victoria, James and Edward, in our shops with the caption 'My mum loves Timpson'.

We were struggling to compete in a crowded shoe retail market, particularly against the powerful and well-run British Shoe Corporation, with their 1,700 shops and 28 per cent share of the market. Emphasising our family connections was a way of giving Timpson a character that couldn't be matched by our biggest competitor.

There was another way to compete. British Shoe, perhaps with some justification, was fairly arrogant, a trait that was reflected in the hard line they took with complaining customers. Shoes get a lot of hard wear and it was inevitable that some fell apart, with about 3 per cent coming back as complaints. But British Shoe gave each shop manager a 2 per cent ceiling on the compensation they could offer, which led to their poor reputation for customer care and tarnished the whole of the shoe retail high street. It was so bad that the Office of Fair Trading (OFT) called on the sector to draw up a Code of Practice to improve standards. Discussions were dragging on when I was appointed to run Timpson, so Stuart Lyons saw our chance to build a reputation as the customer's friend.

We met Sir John Methven, Director General at the OFT, who encouraged us to write and publish our own code ahead of the rest of the trade. It was the perfect opportunity. I relished the task, producing my fair deal promise – 'If you have a good reason to be dissatisfied we will give you your money back' – and creating a labelling system that classified every shoe, boot and slipper into one of six categories from indoor wear to heavy duty and waterproof. Sir John publicly backed my initiative and I got my first real taste of the media, in an interview with Jimmy Young on Radio 2, the BBC's most popular programme.

I soon realised the advantage of fronting the campaign, at a time when the job was usually done by a company spokesman. I didn't need to plug the name of the business and there is no doubt I gained respect by having the courage to put my case personally on a live programme. Although I was naturally a very shy person, I needed to learn how to talk in public. Every business leader has to stand up in front of training sessions and company conferences, and I've learnt that the experience of being thrust behind a microphone gives you more confidence to tackle other public appearances.

Fortunately I have never run a public company, so have never had to bother about the City, but you sense the influence of expensive legal advice when press enquiries have to be directed towards the 'Head of Corporate Affairs' who blocks any probing questions with 'We never comment on market rumours' or 'I have nothing further to add to our official statement'. It's so much better when you get some interesting comments from bosses like Sir Richard Branson and Tim Martin of the pub chain, JD Wetherspoon.

There is a caveat: to be effective you need to have a clear company philosophy. If you believe in values that are in the best interests of both your colleagues and your customers, all you have to do is speak your mind and tell it like it is. If, however, you have a muddled idea of your company strategy and are trying to hide ways in which you are ripping off colleagues and clients, you probably need to hide behind a Director of Corporate Affairs.

Some executives experience paranoid horror if they are told a journalist is on the phone and immediately elect to be 'in a meeting', 'out of the office' or simply 'unavailable'. I pick up the phone. The caller is so surprised to be put straight through to the boss, you have much more chance of getting a fair and sympathetic response.

I started to develop another side to my PR role in 1998. When we were introducing Upside Down Management and the business was starting to expand, I was told we should get someone to write a book about the company. If anyone was going to produce a book I was determined it would be me. As a result I wrote *Dear James*, a book full of lessons to my eldest son based on our successes and failures, bright ideas and momentous mistakes.

I couldn't find a publisher – few authors can – but a magazine, *Real Business*, used extracts to produce a five-page feature and then surprisingly asked me to write an article for the following month. That first article developed into a regular column, which was still appearing eight years later when I was asked to start a business agony column at the back of the magazine. The agony column idea was picked up by the *Daily Telegraph* which, after running some of my answers in a haphazard piece in their Appointments supplement, gave me my own weekly column which has been running for over nine years. The column has become a regular source of comment from customers in our shops all over the country and has spread the word about the way we do business. It has proved to be a great way to promote our name and has led to a fairly full diary of speaking engagements talking to business delegates who also help to spread our story.

By being the public face of the business you are inevitably asked to reveal some parts of your private life. Alex and I took a calculated risk when we agreed to be interviewed for a *Daily Mail* colour supplement feature on our fostering and adoption. I have never regretted that decision, not particularly from a company point of view, although it has done no harm to show that a businessman can have a softer side to his character, but for the good it has done by spreading the word about looked-after children.

I took two more similar risks. First we agreed to be part of a series about millionaires that involved presenter Philip Tibenham interviewing us at home and chasing us across the USA to Vegas. It was worthwhile because Alex was the star of the show and did further good for fostering and adoption. My second, and last, similar programme was *Peter Jones meets …*, a three-part series in which I was one of six entrepreneurs interviewed by Peter Jones from *Dragons' Den*. It helped to explain my maverick way of running the business in contrast to the more traditional methods of the presenter but it also made me feel that we no longer needed any more profile programmes or a series of fly-on-the-wall television. But the best was still to come.

I felt privileged when I was invited to take part in *Desert Island Discs*. The request came three days after Alex's funeral and gave me the perfect opportunity to reflect and select happy memories at a poignant time in my life when it was very important to be positive. Doing the programme with Kirsty Young was more relaxed and enjoyable than anything I had done before. It was very helpful to describe my life with Alex to a much wider audience. But what I hadn't realised was how many people listen to the programme, both live and on podcast. *Desert Island Discs* would be a PR company's dream – it's a good thing that you can't apply to be on the show, you have to be invited.

That programme has led to more media appearances, including *Any Questions* and doing the paper review for BBC Breakfast TV. I now seem to have found my niche. While James does the day-to-day business I run our non-existent PR department. It's a very nice retirement job.

Weekly newsletter

Tell them the figures, publish the latest news
but, most of all, talk about the colleagues.

The weekly newsletter is
part of the 'magic dust' that
creates our culture.

Like my predecessors I had several attempts at producing a company magazine or news sheet but most were sterile management mouthpieces with outdated news that failed to hit the spot.

I have a complete collection of our original company magazine, *The Timpsonian*, that was first published in the 1950s. Today it provides some useful historical background but doesn't give much idea of what life was like for someone who was working on the shop floor. It had statements from the directors, pictures of long-service presentations, a list of retirements and a few obituaries. The news was of new shops and the latest shoe repair machinery but, I suspect, as the magazine only came out three times a year much of the news was out of date. It was an in-house production that followed a standard formula that hardly changed for fifteen years until it moved from black and white to colour.

Our company newsletter changed dramatically in the 1970s when its production was handed over to part of an advertising and promotion agency and the management unashamedly used it to influence employee opinion and promote the importance of the latest company strategy. Rather than reporting company news, the broadsheet outlined future policy and profiled the new faces at the office.

When newsletter production is handed over to an outsider you may get a slicker-looking product, but by using someone who doesn't have a feel for the business there is a risk that you lose a lot of the true company character. Colleagues may not realise that it has been written by an outside journalist and will assume, if the tone of their newsletter has changed, the company is heading in a different direction.

I can understand why most companies pass the newsletter over to their PR company, particularly the glossy sort of publications produced by banks, upmarket estate agents and universities to impress the outside world, but I wonder how many of them are read before being sent for recycling.

For many years I was the editor and writer of our newsletter but never had the time or the talent to produce something good enough or regularly enough, until by pure chance a new idea set me in the right direction. In 1995, shortly after we bought Automagic and our business grew overnight from 220 to 330 shops, I realised that we would have to work hard to keep in touch with all our colleagues if we wanted to continue to feel like a small business.

Every Monday my week started with a list of new problems, often coming in the form of complaints from customers or requests from colleagues. To get my week off to a more positive start I sent every colleague a number of plain slips of paper with the heading 'Dear John – here is some good news'. Next Monday I received fourteen good news notes telling me about record weeks, unusual jobs and famous customers. We put them all on a circular which I sent to every shop. The following week twenty more bits of good news arrived, including one from a colleague whose wife had given birth to twins. Again I sent them all to our shops and singled out the best news of the week, which won an award of £10.

The prize for my good news of the week brought a massive response. I got so much good news on Monday morning I had to leave some out of my weekly circular. The response got even bigger when I had an 'Amaze Me Week' with cash awards of between £5 and £25 for anything that amazed me so much it got printed. Then I ran competitions for the most unusual job, the most famous customer, the biggest single sale and the happiest story of the week.

After a year I had created a bit of a monster which was taking over my office, so we employed someone full time to turn the torrent of good news into a weekly newsletter reporting back to our colleagues everything they were reporting to us. Then I started to add pictures of all the colleagues I met during my shop visits. This gave me the chance to include plenty of people pictures and showed how much we valued the time spent visiting shops. We were getting so many responses from throughout the business it was impossible to put everything on one piece of paper. My cost-conscious colleagues wanted to leave things out but we simply added more pages until some weeks we were filling ten pages of A4.

I always kept my digital camera in my pocket and got the colleagues at every shop to pose for a photograph, but one week we printed the wrong photos. In 2001 I was, on my travels, checking out all our competitor Mr Minit's shops, knowing that an acquisition could be on the cards. One week, unfortunately, instead of publishing pictures of Timpson colleagues, we printed several pictures of the Minit shops I had been stalking. It was an embarrassing error but I got away with it.

My original good news circular finally turned into a newsletter when I started using the front page to keep everyone up to date with events. I've always fancied the idea of being a journalist so I enjoyed thinking up each week's headline. My favourite was the week I used the whole front page to report that six colleagues had been dismissed in the last month for stealing our money – the headline was 'BETRAYED'.

Compiling the newsletter became a full-time job – we employed someone to do nothing else – but it also took a fair slice of my time because I realised it was becoming an integral part of our culture and wanted to make sure it put across the right message. After six years we were still photocopying the news on A4 sheets, and it was time to upgrade. When we changed to a proper printer's format the editorial and production responsibility was outsourced, but to someone who knew the business inside out. Jools Payne, who had advised me on PR for many years, changed roles and has for the last decade produced our weekly *Timpson News*.

We now produce a sixteen-page paper in full colour every week, and Jools is so totally in touch with all parts of our business I know she will print a newsletter that reflects our culture in a publication that is all about Timpson colleagues and the headline company news. Every two or three years we carry out a survey to check colleagues' opinion and the format is regularly changed to keep it fresh and up to date. This is not a cheap exercise: our newsletter costs over £100,000 a year. Although it would be the first thing a keen cost-cutter would axe, I believe it does a great job for the business and represents real value for money. It is worth spending 50p a week per colleague to keep them in touch. I fiercely resist any suggestion that we could save money by going digital – it is so much better to see the news in print.

Regular features include interviews, picture stories of social events and sporting fixtures, news about our company charity, snippets from James's Twitter account, lots of pictures sent in by colleagues, my latest *Telegraph* column and always a full run-down of the sales performance from the previous week with top 10 charts for every sales category. When it comes to the front-page headlines we don't hold back; it is important to let everyone know everything.

We know it works because twenty years after I sent out my first note pads asking for good news, colleagues are still sending in more than enough comments every week to fill a sixteen-page newsletter, and a sure sign that it is being read is when a copy is spotted on the floor of the loo at the back of one of our shops.

Send handwritten letters

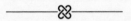

The best way to say 'well done' is
with a proper pen in a letter sent to
the colleague's home address.

Complaint or compliment,
customers always appreciate
a handwritten reply from the boss.

It is a long time since I dictated a letter to a secretary. I have been dragged into the computer age by my grandchildren and learnt how to use an iPhone and an iPad, but despite having an almost illegible scrawl I spend a lot of my time using notepaper and a pen. The internet has put a premium on handwritten letters.

Behind the scenes, in many of our shops, colleagues pin compliments on the wall, messages of personal praise, scribbled on postcards and carefully scripted by hand. By taking the trouble to pick up a pen, people show they sincerely mean what they say. Those letters proudly put on display are proof that proper personal communication really hits the spot.

It's easy to find an excuse to say 'well done' to one of your superstars. When I was our Chief Executive, I wrote a batch of letters every Monday, studying the weekly sales to see if I could spot some record weeks or stunning increases over the previous year. But I soon realised that some colleagues were being congratulated nearly every month, so I kept a record to make sure that my praise was fairly distributed.

I sometimes showed my ignorance by using the wrong name. I should have known better, having been christened William John Anthony Timpson – my friends know me as John, but my doctor's receptionist, most travel agents and letters compiled by computer, all call me William. To avoid making the same mistake, we have a company 'known as' list which tells me the name each Timpson colleague likes to be called.

I spend an hour each month topping and tailing all the long-service letters that accompany certificates to mark one, three, five, ten and every further five years. I sign over 2,500 Christmas cards, send birthday cards to my closest colleagues and write a lengthy Christmas letter of thanks to each of the members of our senior team, but there are two types of letter that I regard as particularly important – Chairman's Awards and letters of condolence.

My Chairman's Award is a gift of cash (usually £100 but has been much more) sent to a colleague to recognise exceptional performance. It is simply a handwritten letter enclosing an after-tax cheque which I send to the colleague's home address. The award has usually been recommended by a line manager or close colleague and when the recipient opens the letter it will come as a complete surprise.

Having received an enormous post bag full of kind comments from friends following the death of my wife, Alex, I know how much messages of sympathy can mean. We are a big family of past and present colleagues who regard me as the head of that family. Letters of condolence usually take quite a lot of time to write, but it gives you the chance to remember the life that has just been lost and put the highlights of your memory down in writing. I was set a superb example when David Cameron wrote to me about Alex. Although my son Edward was one of his Ministers I was amazed that the Prime Minister thought fit to pick up his pen on my behalf.

I also write a lot of letters to customers, always handwritten, usually in response to a complaint or a compliment. My writing might be difficult to read but it does prove that their correspondence hasn't simply been passed to a customer service department. I also send a personal reply to people asking for a charitable donation – the answer is usually 'no' but getting the real reasons for a rejection from the boss is a lot better than a standard reply.

Emails haven't just made proper letters so important – they have also made phone calls much more significant. When a customer complains directly to me in an email that includes all their contact details the best thing to do is pick up the phone and give them a ring. One phone call from the boss can often be all it takes to pacify even the most excitable professional complainer.

Surprise telephone calls can also make a massive impression on your own colleagues. If a star performer completes 25 years' service you will certainly be sending a personal note and probably, like us, invite them to a special long-service presentation, but also consider ringing them up on the exact anniversary date. It is worth making a special effort for special colleagues who will appreciate the personal touch that proves you are a company that really cares about people.

Amazing ways to say
'Well Done!'

The best praise isn't part of a process:
it comes as a total surprise.

**Don't stick to a budget – it's
always worth spending that little
bit more to say well done.**

We have a system to make sure that we recognise long service – with a letter after one and three years plus a cheque every five years. We remember every colleague's birthday by giving them the day off and sending a card. Their boss may well buy an appropriate birthday present, and on the big birthdays we send a bottle of champagne. Our bonus scheme is a way of saying well done with cash every week and we congratulate any colleague who gets married with more champagne, the wedding car and an extra week off.

But you can't give proper praise by following a process – it takes an element of surprise to show you really mean to say well done.

I'm amazed that so many companies feel uncomfortable about handing out compliments. When I was a trustee of the charity ChildLine I was surprised to discover that some volunteers had been answering calls for over fifteen years but never had any recognition for long service or any merit awards. 'We can't use charitable funds to give out awards to staff', I was told. This was one of many excuses I have heard, quoted by people who aren't brave enough to break the mould.

I met a similar problem when I was a trustee at Uppingham School. The Headmaster proudly told the trustees about a highly complimentary inspection report, so I suggested that every member of the common room should get a £250 bonus to say thank you and well done. We had a long debate that raised a number of objections, including 'setting a dangerous precedent' and 'unfair to pay the same amount to the higher paid teachers', but I won the argument and the bonus was paid. 'Don't just add it to their pay', I said, 'send it with personal letters to everyone's home'. Our Chairman looked worried: 'I suppose you expect me to top and tail every letter?' 'Yes', I responded, and that's exactly what he did. The common room was amazed; the different way of saying well done was worth a lot more than £250 a head.

It is a lesson I don't need to teach Steve Docking, the Headteacher at Delamere Primary Academy where I'm a governor. Steve attended our leadership course and has become an expert at Upside Down Management. His maverick approach has included the appointment of a full-time PE teacher, Tom Freeman, who in three years has made a massive contribution to the culture at Delamere. This is one of many ways Steve has used his initiative rather than following the policies and guidelines proposed by local education authorities. To show his appreciation at the end-of-term governors' and staff tea party, Steve gave Tom a surprise award to say thank you. Knowing Tom is an avid Everton fan, he persuaded me to give two of my season tickets for the fixture between Manchester City and Everton, a gesture that showed how well Steve knows his team and understands the impact of both the personal touch and an element of surprise.

The best bits of praise don't stick to the rules, they are individual and often instantaneous.

James shocked us all, in his first few months as our Marketing Director, when he went round the shops with a pocket full of £50 notes handing them out to managers who had record turnover weeks, to a colleague who walked six miles through snow to open a shop, and to another who, as James looked on, dealt brilliantly with an abusive customer with an unjustified complaint. Not everyone was happy – the area teams felt James was undermining their authority and, although he made sure we accounted for the tax, our finance team saw trouble with the taxman. James stopped handing out the £50 notes but, instead, got the area managers to fill their car boots with bottles of wine and boxes of chocolates – instant rewards that didn't have the same stigma.

The wine and chocolates continue, but the area team now have a sophisticated version of £50 in the shape of the Timpson scratch card – a bit like the lottery cards but with Timpson symbols. Scratch the card and you will reveal three keys, three shoes, three watches, three padlocks or three trophies. Everyone wins one of the following prizes: £10, £50, 'A bottle of your choice', 'A meal out on James' or 'The next sale is yours'. James got his way in the end and we now often surprise colleagues by rewarding them with a £50 note.

Once or twice a month I receive a nomination for one of my Chairman's Awards, which take the form of a handwritten letter enclosing a tax-paid cheque always sent to the colleague's home address. But not all awards have to come from the boss – area managers are free to run their own area competitions and organise dinners with area award presentations when they pick their own prizes. But they need to choose the right winners. In the days when the company was small enough for me to attend every area dinner, I remember the tension before our area colleague of the year was announced. As soon as they heard the name you knew whether the area manager had made the right choice – most knew which colleague deserved the prize and greeted the announcement with unprompted applause. But at one dinner the area manager made a bad choice. He was greeted with a stunned silence and we were lucky that fighting didn't break out after dinner. Saying well done is that important.

But you don't have to hold a dinner to hand out accolades: some of the most welcome praise is handed out face-to-face or even down the phone. If a record week is acknowledged by an immediate phone call from the Chief Executive, the shop manager could be walking tall for the rest of the week. One-off gestures like decorating a desk with flowers and balloons on the 30th anniversary of the day a colleague started work for the business is a pretty impressive way to show you appreciate her long service.

Good area managers make a fuss of their star performers and mark birthdays with a carefully picked present in addition to a card (with a note to say thanks for everything over the last year) and the day off on full pay. They know so much about the team it is easy to find a present that will be really appreciated.

One of my own most memorable moments of personal praise was when I invited Brian Armstrong and his wife to come to my office for tea to mark 40 years working with Timpson. Brian was never a high flyer and he faced a few personal challenges but he had a heart of gold, together with a passion for anything to do with John Wayne. As we were finishing our tea and cake I gave Brian an envelope which contained details of a two-week trip to John Wayne's birthplace, Winterset, Iowa. He had a ball, was featured in the local press in the USA and, for the next few years, had a fund of stories to tell his regular customers.

It was the experience with Brian that prompted me to propose a scheme which I called 'Dreams Come True'. Its launch coincided with the year we opened our 1,000th shop and hit £20m gross trading profit for the first time, which for me was a dream come true, so I thought it was a good excuse to turn a few more dreams into reality. It was so popular we now spend about £100,000 a year making at least one colleague's dream come true every month. There have been plenty of long-haul flights to meet long-lost relatives, IVF treatment and complicated dental surgery, chairlifts for mother-in-law and a Christmas trip to Lapland for the kids. We even helped one colleague by funding the legal fees for a tricky divorce from his ex-partner.

My favourites are those that are full of surprise, like the one for John from our shop at the Cross in the centre of Chester who is a dedicated aeroplane spotter and tracks the path of TSR 1, our little company King Air plane, every day it flies. Out of the blue, James fixed it for John to have a day off and go in the plane to Newquay for the day, where he and his partner had lunch at the Jamie Oliver restaurant. The dreams that work best are the things that colleagues think are mission impossible and those that money can't buy. Through 'Dreams Come True', colleagues have been to see the Rolling Stones and the Gold Cup at Cheltenham. Perhaps the best was a scheme plotted to mark the retirement of one of our Regional Managers, Brian Elliot, who was called to a sales conference at Heathrow airport only to find his wife with packed suitcases ready to depart for a surprise holiday in Spain.

I hope that we never stop finding new and amazing ways to say thank you and well done.

Have a great bonus scheme

—❈—

Our weekly bonus scheme creates the
adrenaline that puts a buzz in the business.

**To be successful a bonus
scheme should be simple,
consistent and fair.**

My first real job was working in our shoe shop on Railway Street in Altrincham, just south of Manchester. I vividly remember my first customer, who bought a pair of Tuf boots for 47/9d (about £2.39). I was so nervous, but my anxiety turned to excitement when I put his money in the till. After two weeks all my shyness had disappeared and I was hooked on earning as much commission as possible to supplement my basic wage of £5/17/6d a week (£5.88).

You didn't earn commission on every sale: the company operated what was called a spiff system. We were paid extra cash if we sold the more expensive items or discontinued lines. A pair of Crockett and Jones shoes that sold for 79/11d (£3.99) would earn you a spiff of two shillings (10p), and selling an unpopular pair of last year's fashion shoes could bring in as much as half a crown – 12½p in today's money.

When I had a spell working in our shoe repair factory, part of the Timpson shoe shop in School Road, Sale, I was never going to earn any form of bonus because I was useless at repairing shoes, but the expert cobblers could add 25 per cent to their pay through a piece rate system. Every job they did added one or two extra pence to their pay. It was a scheme copied from our shoe factory in Kettering but wasn't particularly suited to a retail environment where money in the till was more important than the number of jobs done. The bonus arrangements changed dramatically in the mid-1960s.

At first it was all pretty complicated. The weekly target was set by head office, there was a split between sales of merchandise and services and the bonus itself came in two parts – one for the production team and a much smaller amount for the girls who worked behind the counter serving customers. That system led to the simplified scheme we have today.

We use the same calculation in every shop every week. The bonus is based on the wages paid to those people working in the shop during the week – those off sick or on holiday are not excluded. The total wages are multiplied by 4.5 to set the target for that week and we pay a bonus of 15 per cent on all sales over the target with no limit. The payout is split between the colleagues in the shop according to the hours they work and the number of skill points they have accumulated through our training scheme. The money is paid in their next pay packet, as we find that waiting too long reduces the value of the incentive.

No scheme is perfect. It is easier for our colleagues to earn a big bonus in some shops than it is in others, but I have learnt from experience that any tweak intended to make things better won't work. Our colleagues trust, like and understand what we have now. Many companies try to save money by reducing the benefits of their bonus schemes. I would never dare to take that risk – it would break the trust we have with our colleagues.

Our weekly bonus does much more than adding an average of 20 per cent on top of basic pay; it makes a massive difference to the way we do business. Because we pick people with a positive 'go for it' personality, they maximise their bonus by going for extra sales, keeping an eagle eye on staffing levels and making sure they develop their skill level. It isn't surprising that many of our customers think our business is franchised because a lot of our managers think of the shop as their own business.

It's impossible to create a similar incentive scheme for office workers and managers because support colleagues don't have a direct influence on sales, so they view their incentive as a share in success rather than a reward for personal performance.

I've tried a number of ways to link executive pay to

performance. In the 1970s and 80s we had two employee share schemes. They both provided a substantial payout but for the wrong reason: both were involved in a takeover. In 1973 UDS bought William Timpson Ltd and in 1987 I sold the shoe shop business to George Oliver. On each occasion our colleagues picked up a capital sum, but a number were also made redundant.

I know the John Lewis Partnership has based its success on employee ownership, but that doesn't mean it is right for everyone. I don't want to issue any Timpson shares – we prefer to be a 100 per cent owned family business, so we have a scheme for executives that provides a significant percentage of salary, the size depending on our gross profit, which is a supercharged version of the John Lewis partners' dividend. I was determined to be generous, with senior executives having the chance to earn an extra 45 per cent of their salary. Most of our colleagues prefer the reality of a sizeable share in success, to the long-term possibility of the capital gain a share scheme can bring.

In developing the scheme I made plenty of mistakes. I started by deciding how much bonus I would like everyone to earn if we hit budget, but it is foolish for anyone to think that they can forecast profit. In the first year of my scheme we had a fantastic year and everyone got the maximum payment. The business was growing quickly so I set a stiffer target for the following year. We failed so miserably to meet my forecast that the new formula would have paid out nothing. I couldn't leave my hard-working team empty-handed so we ignored the formula and gave everyone half of the big maximum payout they had received in the first year.

You will never set the perfect bonus target, but you can gain from experience and use a bit of common sense. Our executive bonus scheme has survived for over ten years by using the following guidelines:

1. If the target is set so low that everyone gets the maximum bonus, when paying out in full, make two points: a) Don't expect to earn as much next year; and b) Don't spend it all at once.
2. Wait until you are at least two months into the new bonus year before you set the next target and announce the new scheme.
3. If you have an unexpectedly bad year, don't stick to the formula – pay a bonus big enough to be fair and fully satisfy your conscience.

Like every other part of management, setting the rules for a bonus scheme is an art not a science, but always aim to be fair, err on the side of generosity and never aim to save money by changing the rules to reduce the bonus bill.

Celebrate success

---❧---

Never forget the people who made it happen on your behalf.

You can always find an excuse to have a party.

You never know when misfortune can turn out to be a massive piece of luck. In 1969 our shoe shop in Grove Street, Wilmslow, caught fire. No one was injured but all the stock was damaged by smoke. We never discovered the cause – it might have started in the shoe repair factory – but sadly the biggest loss was suffered by the wine merchant, Owens, next door. Their shop was unaffected but the fire service poured so much water onto the blaze it flooded the wine cellar and most of the soggy labels were detached from the bottles, so without a tasting it was impossible to distinguish premier cru from vin ordinaire.

Our shoe shop closed for over a week, with a big poster on the window: 'Fire Sale Starts Friday 10am'. When the time came there was a significant queue. Luckily the shop had a rear door leading to a small car park so we could slip extra stock in every night to keep the sale going. The shop took serious money and cleared a lot of redundant stock. Although we felt sorry for the wine merchant, it wasn't such a bad fire after all.

That fire gave me an idea. When I returned, as Managing Director, to Timpson in 1975, we had a mountain of slow-moving stock and my Chairman, Stuart Lyons, was keen to promote our status as a family business. I successfully announced our 110th birthday in a television advert: 'TIMPSON ... Timpson are 110 and to celebrate we are offering 110 pence off 110 styles.' Then, for our July Sale I shut every store before advertising on Tuesday and Wednesday night: 'Our shops are closed to prepare for the biggest ever shoe sale that starts on Thursday at 10am.'

By 8.30am, on that Thursday, I was in Sheffield where we had five shoe shops in the city centre. It was a nervous 90 minutes. I walked quickly from shop to shop but nothing was going on. Our shops were, as instructed, all shut, the windows were covered with sale posters but passers-by appeared to take no notice. At 9.45am I saw a potential customer waiting patiently outside our shop in the Haymarket, five minutes later there were four more and by 10.00am the queue stretched the length of our shop and round the corner. We let in a few at a time and kept a queue outside all morning. The same thing was happening all over the country. The sale was a stunning success: in only three days we beat our record week.

This showed the benefits of a bit of drama and that customers are interested in company history, so when we redesigned the shoe repair shops in 1995 I put 'established 1903' on the fascia. To be honest 1903 was a bit of a guess, but it was close enough to the date when Timpson started repairing shoes and 2003 seemed a good year to celebrate our centenary. We had a centenary dinner in a marquee at my home, with Centenary Awards, and to mark our special year we gave every colleague their birthday off.

It has never been difficult to find an excuse to celebrate. As we were raising money for the NSPCC at the time, I persuaded the Duke of Westminster to come to our Millennium Awards lunch in January 2000 with 135 colleagues from across the UK who had been nominated across several categories. We have celebrated my 50 years with the business and 150 years since my great grandfather started his first shop (when we took 150 colleagues for a five-day celebration in Malta). The parties, most in a marquee in my garden, have also included our version of the television show *Stars in Their Eyes* and a highly professional *Timpson's Got Talent*. Celebrating success is a great way to create fun. In 2013 when we opened our 1,000th shop we made sure it was the pod outside Tesco in Baguley, built on the site which was previously the Timpson shoe warehouse.

For 25 years I have held regular suppliers' lunches, when I

take the opportunity to give people closely linked to our business a frank update on company progress, thank them for their support and award trophies to several Suppliers of the Year. Nearly all our celebrations include a few prizes. Our area managers' conferences involve very few conference sessions because most of the time is spent on physical challenges – abseiling, orienteering, go-karting – but there is always time for a prize-giving.

Our colleagues don't have to wait for a marquee to appear in my garden – they are free to celebrate their individual successes at any time. Area managers run a social programme and every night out or day spent paintballing provides the chance to present a few prizes. They don't even have to wait for a social event. If a manager has achieved a record week or gone way beyond the call of duty, the area team can make a special award, which might be an extra day's paid holiday plus a celebration meal out.

We are often invited to enter national business awards. Many are thinly disguised PR campaigns on behalf of an accountancy firm or bank, aimed at gathering lots of potential clients together (at the clients' expense) and providing a lucrative night for the hotel where a table for ten costs £1,500. I much prefer our in-house events but can't ignore the joy shown by the winning team when their name is announced. Everyone likes to work for a company that is recognised as being a winner.

Celebrating is easy when things are going well, but when a company is struggling, profits are down, costs are being cut and there is talk of redundancy, celebrating success becomes even more important. Despite making less profit, plenty of people will have done some amazing and heroic things that shouldn't be missed. You might have a more modest marquee, but, even in the darkest days, you must continue to celebrate success.

Keep looking for new ideas

Over half the things that will make us money
twenty years from now have yet to be invented.

Keep wandering round with
your eyes wide open – you
never know where the next
idea will come from.

During my time buying ladies' shoes, before 1973, I had to be constantly on the latest trend. Each season the bestseller would be a style that customers had never seen before. Luckily the best place to go to research the latest fashion was Italy, so every June I spent a week studying the shoe shop windows and what the girls were wearing in Rome, Florence, Verona and Venice. By observing Italian flair and ingenuity, my eye was kept in step with the steadily turning fashion cycle, and I was shown the importance of looking out for new ideas.

Other retailers probably never realised how they contributed to the development of Timpson. The flags that fly outside most of our shops advertising key cutting or watch repairs were copied from Dixons in the 1970s (we still call them the Dixon flag). Our key cutting sales doubled in the mid-1970s as soon as we introduced a window display technique, copied from Richard Shops, and we started to make engraving a serious service after I saw the key and engraving 'Can do Bars' on a trip to the west coast of America in 1987. Very few ideas are original and hardly any are discovered while you are sitting behind a desk.

Most ideas that have changed our business start in one of our shops, when a colleague has the courage to have a go at something new. Prize for our most profitable idea must go to the first colleague (we don't know who it was) who decided to offer to cut a second key for half price. Few customers need a second key, but when asked, most want one. 'Second key half price' is such an obvious winner we quickly abandoned any thoughts of it being a special offer and made it a permanent promotion – it has been running for 34 years!

The freedom we give our colleagues to use their initiative is a great way to discover new ideas. Our lifetime guarantee on watch batteries was developed by the area team in Yorkshire after one shop had started offering customers the extended guarantee at premium price. In canny Yorkshire fashion they kept the idea to themselves for long enough to outperform the rest of the company before sharing the scheme with all the other area managers.

My son James found our latest idea in China, where he was discussing the development of a Timpson franchise. There are a lot of shoe repairers in China but most are unsophisticated workbenches that look like a temporary market stall. We thought they had a lot to learn from us but didn't expect to pick up a new trick from them. James was amazed to discover that far and away the biggest part of the cobblers' service in China is shoe washing – restoring old and smelly trainers to their former glory. We are soon about to see whether there is a similar demand in the UK.

Every acquisition has the potential to reveal a new source of turnover. In 1987, the small twelve-shop chain Shoetech taught us how to increase shoe repair sales by always introducing a sole and heel job – 'heels are free if you have the soles done now'. Once our colleagues realised what a difference this could make to their bonus, sales increased significantly. Automagic, the 110-shop chain we bought in 1995, showed us the profit to be made out of umbrellas, particularly in central London, when the shop in Cannon Street station sold £2,000 worth of umbrellas between 8.00 and 9.00 one Tuesday morning.

Each year we seem to set out with even more ideas than the year before, and it is a good thing that we manage to find a constant flow of new ways to grow the business because most of the things we will be doing to make money twenty years from now have yet to be invented.

Some people get in the way of good ideas. These

progress-blockers broadly split into two camps: the 'Ah Buts' and the 'Gunnas'. The 'Ah Buts' go to great lengths to find reasons why new things can't be done and, if done, are doomed to failure. The 'Gunnas' pretend to be enthusiastic, and are always 'going to' (gunna) do it, but find a list of excuses to delay implementation. There are lots of people who don't like change. Three years ago I dreamt up and designed some new graphics for our shops. It was a bold move: I replaced the interior signs that advertised our services with graphics that talked about our culture, including our holiday homes and birthdays off. I first saw them displayed in a shop when I called at Bramhall, where our manager made it quite clear that he wasn't pleased. 'Have you seen these?' he said, pointing at the new posters. 'What clever idiot at the office has thought up this stupid idea?' I kept quiet, though I'm pleased to say the massive interest our customers have taken in the graphics about our culture speaks for itself.

You seldom, if ever, see game-changing ideas submitted to a suggestion scheme, and I'm always wary of outsiders who propose to come and see me to offer (for a fee) a groundbreaking new service that would transform our business. We have tried a few – spectacle repairs, buying gold, recycling mobile phones and even offering pay day loans, but none of them worked and despite being in the while-you-wait service business, we turned down the chance to do tattooing and ear piercing.

Most proposers of an add-on service point out that all we have to do to make a fortune is to take an extra £100 per shop per week. But life is not that easy. We thought we were on a winner when we started repairing mobile phones and quickly spent £350k on the stock and kit to put the service in every shop – big mistake. You should never put a new idea into all the shops at once. Start slowly in a few branches, learn lots of lessons and when you know what you are doing, spread it to the rest of the business. The impatience with which we attacked the mobile phone market cost us a lot of money and delayed the proper development of what is now proving to be an important addition to our business, by at least two years. I made matters worse by naming one of my wife Alex's racehorses 'Pretty Mobile' to celebrate our initial flurry of success. It was another decision that went wrong: the horse is very pretty but not particularly mobile.

We didn't make the same mistake with watch repairs, a service which was prompted in 1996 by Glenn Edwards, then a branch manager in West Bromwich. Before joining us, Glenn had worked with a watch repairer, so he started to offer his Timpson customers a watch strap and battery service, taking £100 a week. When I visited his shop I discovered what Glenn was doing and we put the service in four more shops, and total takings on watch repairs reached £500 a week. We now offer the service nationwide with a total turnover of £25m a year.

Give new ideas a good chance of working by starting off in a small way, but carry out your trials in the places and with the people who are most likely to make them work. ('If it doesn't work there it won't work anywhere' is a much better approach than 'If it works there it will work anywhere'.)

As a shoe buyer I went to Italy, but to find ideas for today's Timpson I simply stay in the UK touring the shops, talking to our colleagues who have taught me how to develop our business. But I may be travelling much further afield, especially if the Timpson name gets established in China. The prospects are enormous: one study suggests the market could support over 20,000 shops with at least 1,000 in Beijing alone. But we will start by opening no more than five shops. However good and however big the idea, it is always wise to start in a small way and work out what works best before embarking on a big programme of investment.

There is no rush – take time to find the winning formula before investing a lot of money in your latest route to success.

Have a 'Happy Index'

———— ⚫ ————

*Get colleagues who run your business to tell
you how well the business is running.*

**Our Happy Index is the
best way we've found to
measure the success of
Upside Down Management.**

I am still embarrassed to admit that over 40 years ago I used to carry out formal staff appraisals, faithfully following the format laid down by our HR Director. I asked the necessary questions including, 'What do you think have been your major achievements over the last year?' and 'Do you feel you have had all the support you need?' They were awkward conversations, not helped by the fact that I didn't like doing them and most team members didn't want to either. I tried to find an area of weakness where our star performer could improve, and made a point of giving a word of encouragement by praising even the most hopeless colleague who should in truth have been encouraged to leave.

I now see the appraisal programme as a massive waste of management time that drains energy from the organisation and diverts attention from the main purpose of the business. I did my last round of appraisals in 1982 and never want to do another. A good boss should know when it is time to have a personal chat with a member of the team and every one of our colleagues has the right to meet their boss whenever they want to talk. Managing people can't be reduced to a box-ticking process.

Our success depends on the management team providing front-line colleagues with the support they need and removing any obstacles that get in the way of their success. The most important measurement is, therefore, how front-line colleagues rate the quality of support they receive.

We took part in the first survey of 'Best Places to Work' compiled on behalf of the *Sunday Times*, and were regularly placed in the top ten, on the basis of a questionnaire completed by our colleagues. We stopped entering many years ago, partly because they introduced an entry fee but mainly because we discovered that Timpson colleagues didn't like completing the detailed questionnaire. We learnt a big lesson: if you want your colleagues to cooperate with a survey, make it simple. That thinking led to our Happy Index.

Every year we ask all our branch colleagues one question: 'On a scale of 1 to 10, how do you rate your area team?' – just one question, but there is plenty of space to add comments. By making it simple we get a better than 90 per cent return rate and the comments give us a clear idea when things are working well and where there could be a problem.

The Happy Index has been so successful it is now part of the way we run the business. Most management initiatives, like suggestion schemes and special bonus arrangements, seldom last for very long, but the Happy Index isn't just an annual fixture in our calendar – it is also used to measure the service provided by every department, including buying, warehouse, finance and our watch repair workshop.

I like the fact that it is our own people measuring our own performance. A survey carried out by outsiders would find it difficult to home in on the real things that matter to our business. At the heart of our formula for success is the principle that managers do the job by giving their team all the support they need. The Happy Index measures how well we are running the business.

Perfect Day

*We never had a good way to
promote good housekeeping until
we found the answer at Asda.*

**People can't be perfect
every day, but everyone can
be perfect once a year.**

The colleagues who ran our first shops weren't really shopkeepers. They were craftsman cobblers used to being in a workshop who were moved into our shops and put on public view. Originally housekeeping wasn't much of a problem because customers were always served by counter girls who managed the merchandise and tidied the shop. But when shoe repair demand fell we couldn't afford to pay people who didn't sole shoes or cut keys so the cobblers had to do it all, which included keeping a tidy shop. We no longer employed a junior lad who could be delegated to do the dusting.

It was difficult to change the habits of a lifetime, so despite our attempts to raise standards our cobblers were reluctant to use a vacuum cleaner, continued to put a scruffy work apron over their T-shirt and jeans, smoked cigarettes while they worked, read the newspaper if there was no work to do, and nipped to the pub for two pints of beer every lunchtime. The senior executive and area managers tried to improve standards by running their finger along the interior pelmets to detect dust and sending a damning memo to any manager whose shop could be regarded as 'a tip'. But no one expected shoe repairers to be smart – these were factories on the high street so noise, smells and dirt were a normal part of a cobbler's shop.

I tried to make a difference when I got seriously involved in our shoe repair business. In 1979, Mike Frank, the general man-ager, was away for several weeks on a residential management course (in those days we thought a dose of management theory was the best way to develop our senior team). Mike was a class operator who kept our shoe repair business in profit during a traumatic period for the industry, but he and his small senior team kept the rest of us at a decent distance, and it was difficult to influence the way they worked. While Mike was away I visited a lot of his shops and, while enjoying the company of the colleagues I met, couldn't help noticing the poor standards of personal appearance and housekeeping. 'But all shoe repairers are the same', I was told. That, to me, made a campaign for better standards even more important. I argued that if we could raise our game we would stand out from all our competitors. I also put it another way by suggesting that if customers saw we cared about the look of our shops they would also believe that we would take good care of their shoes.

I introduced a uniform with an apron and a shirt that had always to be worn with the Timpson tie. The tie became more than a token gesture – it was the one thing beyond everything else that distinguished us from every other cobbler. The new uniform was introduced at the same time as our first major housekeeping campaign.

This new wave of cleanliness didn't last long, as I was soon to discover when I went with my wife, Alex, to visit our shop in Asda near Reading while on the way to a wedding one Saturday morning. We had been there barely 30 seconds and I was just starting to check the sales figures when Alex declared: 'This place is filthy.' Then, turning to the poor young trainee who was still waiting for his manager to arrive, she asked him: 'Have you got a hoover?' He sheepishly lifted his vacuum cleaner out of a cupboard but admitted he had never had a go. Alex grabbed the machine and gave a masterclass in how to clean a carpet. Just at that point the manager came round the corner, took one look and shot off to the Asda cafe until the coast was clear.

After that visit, Alex was on a mission and appointed herself unpaid Timpson Housekeeping Champion. At our next area managers' conference Alex, together with June Kent, who cleaned our home, ran a 45-minute session that included how to hoover a carpet and the proper way to use a duster. I am sure it made a difference but even the force of Alex's personality was not enough to really raise our standards on the high street.

We never gave up. A poster was put behind the scenes of every shop full of cleaning tips, together with a routine to be followed at the beginning and end of every day. We supplied every shop with an 'emergency toolkit' that included cleaning materials, some new aprons and a few spare ties. At one point, if we spotted a particularly untidy shop, we allocated an extra colleague who would stay until standards improved (that was an expensive solution but it worked well because the presence of an extra team member dramatically reduced the resident team's usual level of bonus earnings). I found another ploy that made a difference. If I visited a shop that was a real tip, I took a number of photos, sent them to the area manager and asked him to send me his pictures when he was proud of the way the shop was presented.

We kept coming up with housekeeping ideas, because we knew how much it mattered. But despite all our efforts our shops were not that much cleaner than the competitor down the road, though at least with luck our guys were wearing a tie. Even when I told everyone that the first of our only two rules was to 'Look the part', I knew that there was still a big difference between Alex's dream and the reality that she would see if she ever visited a shop.

We found the answer during a half-day visit to an Asda store where James and I had a backstage tour. That was when we heard about their Perfect Day, the one day in the year when every store was expected to be perfect. We grabbed the idea with glee and within six months Timpson had its first Perfect Day, with a prize for the best turned-out branch. We knew it would work a month before the day itself arrived. Suddenly shop colleagues were ordering replacement posters, discarding dirty aprons and overhauling the vacuum cleaner. People whose daily housekeeping was haphazard relished the idea of putting everything in the proper place for one perfect day a year.

Two years later the idea was introduced into our office. In 2007 James and I went to Helsinki to visit Sol, a commercial cleaning company that had a bizarre central office built in an old film studio. It had wacky graphics and an eccentric layout but it was immaculate, not a file or a piece of paper to be seen, and James loved it so much that within a month we had plans for a dramatic makeover at Timpson House, with a new uncluttered culture that made my desk the untidiest in the building.

Introducing the concept of a perfect day into Timpson House was an obvious move, but we hadn't expected what happened next. When the Perfect Day arrived after a week when three skips were filled with rubbish, everyone dressed up for the special day. Our finance department won top prize with every team member kitted out for a wedding. The day was more than perfect, it produced a buzz that put morale on an all-time high and led to more makeover days. During the 2014 FIFA World Cup, departments drew lots to decide which finalist they represented and decorated their office to depict their country. The development department built a ten-foot stack of pizza cartons (the leaning tower of Pisa) and dressed up as gondoliers to represent Italy, but they were easily beaten by the customer support team who were all geisha girls in full costume and fantastic make-up, which secured the top prize for Japan.

It still works. The Perfect Day has a permanent place in the Timpson calendar and although we know our housekeeping can still be a bit patchy, at least it is pretty perfect on one day every year.

Communicate in pictures

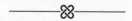

People find it easier to read
pictures rather than words.

It takes a long time to write
a short book that gets the
message across using as
few words as possible.

In 1995, we had just added 110 shops by buying Automagic and I was prompted to check how the team were going to communicate the quality standards we expected, particularly for shoe repairs, to our new colleagues. I was in for a surprise. 'We don't have any specific standards', said Mike Donaghue, our shoe repair product manager. 'Everyone is simply expected to produce a good commercial job.' 'But how does anyone know what that looks like?' I asked. 'Good question', said Mike. 'But it's the way we have done it for years – experienced shoe repairers teach the new starters and Timpson standards have been passed down from one generation to the next.' That might have worked in the old days but it didn't seem like a good way to set standards for our newly acquired shops.

I had an idea. 'Don't go anywhere', I said to Mike, 'I will be back in fifteen minutes.' I went to the local garden centre where I bought a book, one I remembered from my early attempts to grow vegetables. It is a simple-to-read guide written by Dr D.G. Hessayon, full of pictures that make it easy to follow. 'That's what we need', I told Mike on my return, 'our own illustrated shoe repair guide.' I started writing it ten days later, during an Easter weekend, four days of continuous heavy rain.

My aim was to use as few words as possible and get the pictures to tell the story. It should have been an impossible task as I'm no good at drawing and can't repair a shoe. But the lack of cobbling knowledge was an advantage because having spoken to the experts I was able to describe each step in words and pictures that a novice would understand. The drawing problem was saved by Robert Barrow, a flexible working colleague based in Blackpool, who has now been illustrating my books for nearly twenty years.

The shoe repair guide worked, so, to prepare for the next manual I attended several key cutting courses. We soon had an illustrated guide for key cutting, then all our other services were put into pictures and became the basis of our training programme and skill qualifications.

Next James, our Chief Executive, gave me a different challenge. 'Can we teach our management style in pictures in a similar way to the skill manuals?' In the 1970s I wrote two storybooks for use in the children's departments of our shoe shops: *Maud the Measuring Gauge* and *Freddie Flip Flop*. They were similar to the *Mr Men* books, a format I used for the first management book, *How to be a Great Boss*, which again used pictures with as few words as I could get away with. This was the first of a set of management books that includes *How to Pick Great People*, *How to Create a Great Team* and *How to be a Great Big Boss*.

The format of using few words and lots of pictures doesn't just work for business books. I had a lot of fun writing *How to Play Golf Quickly*, and I hope some of the ex-offenders who join us benefit from *How to Create a Career After Prison*, but my most significant picture book was one written to help adoptive families.

During our time as foster carers and the parents of adopted children, Alex and I sometimes struggled to understand how to cope with some quite challenging behaviour. Life became much easier once we understood about attachment theory, which explains how the lack of the normal bond with an adult in the first few years of childhood can lead to lack of security, trust and confidence which in turn causes children, as they grow up, to challenge the world around them. There are plenty of books written about attachment but they are all quite difficult for most people to understand. They are probably clear to academics but we needed to get the message across to ordinary people looking after these children. It was the perfect topic for another little *Mr Men*-type book, *A Guide to Attachment*. Over 100,000 copies have been distributed (they are now available free in our shops and from our website) and a special version for schools, *Looking After Looked After Children*, is also available for free with the hope that attachment theory will become part of initial teacher training throughout the UK.

If you want to get a message across, it is important to remember that pictures talk louder than words.

The Residential

We *teach colleagues how to cut keys and repair watches, but we also make sure they get the culture.*

At the Residential they discover we really do run the business upside down.

Although, every three years, we carry out our cash for growth cost-cutting campaign, we never save money by reducing our commitment to training. Without skill training we wouldn't have a business. We make our money by providing a service, but we don't look for qualified craftsmen, we recruit people with personality and then teach them how to do the job. Everyone who joins us starts as an apprentice, and is expected to reach our basic skill level in all the main Timpson services within sixteen weeks.

Our apprenticeship nearly all happens out in the field. Each area has a training manager who makes sure the trainees work alongside an experienced colleague who can teach by example and guide them through our technical manuals, which are written in pictures rather than words. To graduate as a qualified branch colleague they must pass a series of skill tests, monitored by the area training manager. There is a big incentive to learn, because every extra skill point means a bigger share of the weekly branch bonus.

Although skill training is at the centre of the way we do business, we don't and probably never will qualify for any government training grants. Sadly, we don't tick the official boxes – there is no NVQ for key cutting or shoe repairs, you can't go to a Cobblers' College, the only place in the UK you can learn the skills of our trade is at Timpson. But far from showing us the nation's gratitude for training just about every qualified shoe repairer in the country, we are required to pay the government's new apprenticeship levy in full and get nothing back. That is the end of my rant, because I prefer to pay up and continue to run a training scheme that works really well for our colleagues and customers.

Despite ignoring the advice of outside training providers, we reckon that we have our apprenticeship sorted, but the most important bit has nothing to do with skills. It is essential that we ensure every new colleague gets our culture, and to get the message home, all new starters attend our Residential Course at Timpson House.

We can teach technical skills out in the field, but, despite the books we have written about Upside Down Management, the only way to explain our unusual culture is to tell colleagues face-to-face. That is the way to emphasise that we really do pick people with personality and trust them with the freedom to use their initiative.

New colleagues normally come on the Residential after they have been with the company over three months. We run a course every four to six weeks and with the company growing rapidly there tend to be around 55 participants on each course.

At first I had a few worries, because I recalled the problems we encountered in the 1970s when most colleagues who attended our training courses stayed at what we called the Timpson hostel, a large house nearby, on the border between Altrincham and Bowdon, which is now a nursing home. The success of many of the courses was marred by the behaviour back at the hostel – it was a mistake to mix men on a shoe repair course with young girls attending a three-day session on customer service.

Today our delegates stay in a local hotel and, fortunately, we seldom suffer from any social incidents, although there are still colleagues whose behaviour brings their career to an end when it has only just begun.

It helps to have a big crowd from all over the country. Most come by train or car but there are always a few who fly in from Scotland or Ireland. They all come with a hint of trepidation, but quickly discover that they are surrounded by similar characters. We tell them at the start that they have one thing in common with each other: they are all rated 9 or 10 out of 10.

The Residential runs from a Wednesday lunchtime until the following afternoon and every minute is masterminded by Peter Harris, our Training Manager. He not only makes sure that he gets the culture message across, but he also makes it fun. The colleagues are split into teams so a competitive element runs throughout the two days. During the tour of our office and warehouse each group has to observe carefully so that they can answer a series of quiz questions. In the evening, dinner is followed by a number of games which all score points for the team.

Either James or myself spend about an hour with every Residential. We start by going round the room asking each colleague where they are working – then we tell them some facts about their shop. We want to demonstrate the importance we attach to visiting shops and knowing the detail. Once we have spoken to everyone, we start the session by talking about Upside Down Management. Once we have set the scene we leave it to Peter Harris and his team to do the rest.

It works. The feedback is fantastic. Colleagues who came with reluctance and a few nerves go home full of enthusiasm, having found out much more about our business and, for many, having met some new friends.

Training is so important to our business that we are planning to rebuild our training centre and rename it the Timpson University. It will offer a range of skill and management courses on locksmith work, interview techniques, mobile phone technology and how to provide special support to colleagues who join us from prison. But at the new Timpson University the most important course will always be the Residential. Every business should take time explaining the company culture to new starters.

The Annual Report

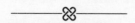

*Your colleagues and their families ought
to be told as much as possible about
the business that pays their salary.*

**A lot of companies are too
secretive for their own good.**

In the late 1970s I was part of the Footwear Working Party set up by the government as part of the National Economic Development Council. The shoe trade was singled out because UK manufacturers were suffering in the face of fast-increasing imports, jobs were being lost and factories closed down. As one of the three retailers on a committee of over twenty people who mainly represented manufacturers, unions and government, I was expected to produce some new ways to support British suppliers. It was a pretty futile mission, since most British shoe manufacturers were finding it impossible to withstand foreign competition, but in the 1970s over 100,000 people were working in UK shoe factories. It is now well under 10,000. But I was keen to do my bit and stunned a somewhat cynical industry by running a series of open days when any UK-based manufacturer was invited to view the samples we had selected from abroad. By seeing the latest styles at such competitive prices, they started to understand why so much business was going overseas.

I have been as open as possible with our suppliers ever since. For the last 25 years I've hosted a succession of suppliers' lunches which have always included my no-holds-barred report on our company performance and future plans, followed by the presentation of a number of trophies to our Suppliers of the Year. Other companies have been known to give their suppliers a free lunch but use the occasion to demand that their guests pay for the experience by giving a bigger discount or extended credit. I don't believe that bullies succeed in business. Suppliers should be seen as business partners who are part of your team. You will make the most money together if both feel they are working on the same side. Exactly the same principle applies to the relationship with employees, which is why I believe in telling our colleagues everything I possibly can about our business and, once a year, reveal all they need to know in our Annual Report.

I don't understand why most companies are so paranoid about keeping all the facts and figures confidential. Shop assistants working for a big high street chain are very unlikely to be told how much money their shop is taking and how the performance compares with last year. I even find in our franchise, Snappy Snaps, that a few of the franchisees refuse to let their employees see the numbers. Perhaps they fear that if the figures are good, their employees will want a wage rise, but it doesn't work like that. Knowing the sales performance is an essential ingredient in creating a buzz; turnover is our measure of success and we want colleagues to know that they are part of a winning team.

I write the Annual Report myself, and it is one the jobs during the year that makes me really think about the business. I use as many pictures and as few words as possible but put in plenty of figures. The Timpson Annual Report bears little resemblance to the sort of report produced by a plc. The company reports produced for shareholders are so full of information they communicate nearly nothing. When I thumb through the pages of standard statements and obscure schedules printed to satisfy accountancy standards I'm bewildered. Not just because I don't understand what a lot of it is about, but bewildered that intelligent people have allowed the system to develop to a stage where the main beneficiaries are the lawyers, accountants and printers. If an annual report is meant to be a clear statement to shareholders of company affairs, reports in the current format completely fail to fit the bill. The only chance of returning to clarity and common sense is to scrap all the present accountancy standards and start all over again.

Fortunately, when I write my report I don't have to stick to anyone else's guidelines. As a private company, although we must file our accounts we don't have to publish them. But I think every colleague has the moral right to know as much as possible about the health of the business that plays such a big part in their and their families' lives.

It is very important not to fudge the figures. I want all our colleagues to see the same numbers that are presented in the annual accounts to our Board of Directors. I back the figures up with my one-page written report which tries to highlight the main events of the year. The rest of the report is told in pictures, with pages given to our investment programme, acquisitions, charity work carried out by the Timpson Foundation, colleagues' personal successes, landmarks and appointments, news of our colleague support programme including new holiday homes and the most special dreams we have made come true, new services, new training courses and lots of pictures of colleagues who have made a real difference.

I hope my Annual Report goes way beyond the figures. It is the story of another year in the life of the family of colleagues who make up our business and it is written mainly with them in mind. I send a copy to every colleague – it goes to their home. In my covering letter I encourage everyone to show the report to the rest of their family, who are dependent on our success, and I also suggest showing it to their friends. I like to think our colleagues are proud of the part they play in our achievements.

Most of all, our Annual Report talks about, and is an important part of, our company culture.

Never make decisions
at a meeting

———— ⋇ ————

The best decisions are made in private
and confirmed at a meeting.

Non-executives shouldn't
make executive decisions.

I wonder how much time Britain spends in meetings. Trains are full of people travelling to and from meetings. Call someone on the telephone and they are often said to be in a meeting. Attempts to arrange a meeting can be met with 'Can't do it then, I've got back-to-back meetings all day'. Their diary is almost full before the year begins with Board meetings, subsidiary boards, standing committees, monthly review meetings, the Monday morning discussion meeting, appraisals, budget meetings, trade association council meetings, forward-planning away days, succession-planning and salary review meetings and probably a meeting to discuss the future schedule of meetings.

The agenda will be sent out, an information pack be prepared, some people travel a fair distance, a few stay at a hotel and to make their journeys worthwhile, the meeting takes over four hours, before the secretary writes minutes which few people ever read. Meetings can soak up so much of the working week there is little of it left to do any work.

Running a business by committee and having meetings can become a dangerous addiction. Meetings held for the right reasons are an important part of day-to-day business. By getting together, managers can discuss ideas, communicate decisions, debate issues and draw on their joint expertise, but managers who spend most of their working life in a meeting room don't know enough about their business.

Like all forms of addiction, meetings have the ability to gradually take over an organisation. To guard against death by committee, Asda discourage long-winded discussion by having a meeting room without any chairs. At Timpson, all our meeting rooms are behind glass so we can all see who are huddled together.

Despite my dislike of conference tables, I recognise that meetings have a part to play. Fortunately, for the last 30 years, I have usually been chairing the meetings I attend, so if we stray from the point or go on too long I have only myself to blame. Being in the chair gives you the chance to keep control but it also brings a duty to prepare properly by reading the papers (I normally read them twice) and picking out the points that really need to be discussed. As the chairman, it is important to give everyone the chance to contribute but you must also stop people who hijack the discussion by talking about irrelevant or insignificant topics.

It is odd, in the modern world of instant communication and high-speed travel, that so many things take so long. I reckon that a round of golf should take no more than three and a half hours, a dinner party should be over in three, and every meeting completed in less than two. My wife, Alex, never stayed in a meeting longer than an hour. Fortunately I have seldom been involved in all-day meetings that break for lunch.

As chairman, I've always felt the responsibility for finishing the meeting as soon as possible, but sometimes discovered that such brevity isn't popular with every committee member. My first appointment as a chairman was for a Citizens' Advice Bureau area committee. I hadn't realised that, for some of the delegates, the annual general meeting was a major event of their year and they particularly looked forward to a friendly debate discussing any other business. When I completed the agenda in 35 minutes I was greeted with a hostile silence.

I am prouder of my performances when chairing the finance and general purposes committee at Uppingham School, where, by easily beating my two-hour target I was able, after one meeting, to watch Alex's horse run in the 1.35 at Uttoxeter, and, after another, got to the Etihad stadium in time to see Manchester City kick off at 3.00pm against Aston Villa.

On the positive side, Board meetings have a hidden benefit, by providing a useful ploy during negotiations – 'I will need a better offer before I can recommend it to the Board', or 'We must have everything agreed before Friday's Board meeting'.

It was a tense Timpson Board meeting, one of my first as a director, that taught me never to take a decision at a meeting. During a discussion about window displays and advertising, the debate somehow became critical of the marketing manager and the decision was made that he should be made redundant. On a whim he was about to lose his job and I couldn't sleep, thinking about it. Luckily the meeting was held on a Friday and I was able to contact my fellow directors over the weekend and reverse the decision before it was put into practice.

Non-executive directors shouldn't take executive decisions. Governors do not run a school, they support and advise the Headteacher. Company directors have a similar relationship with their Chief Executive. The Board are responsible for hiring and if necessary, firing their top manager but they should never tell the Chief Exec what to do. The Board can give guidance, offer expertise, ask awkward questions and discuss all the options, but no vote should be taken and no decisions should be made. The business isn't run by the Board – the buck should always stop with the executive team.

Stick to what you know

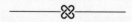

Success in one business doesn't mean you have the skills to be successful elsewhere.

Thoroughly understand how and why you make your money.

Every year a few people ask me: 'I want to run my own business, how do I start?' I always tell them to start with a hobby, something that interests them and they are good at. If your sole objective is to create a business, it is almost certainly doomed to failure. Businesses are created by ideas – it seldom works if you first decide to build a business and then look for the idea to make it work. Don't be fooled by the bankers who put such emphasis on having a business plan. Business plans don't create a business, they are simply written to secure investment for a business idea that has already shown early signs of success.

I've made several theoretical and hopeless leaps into the dark. The first was called Shoetique, an imaginative idea in 1969 which, for the first time, put fashion clothing into a shoe shop. I started by buying some dresses and separates to sell in the ladies' shoe department which was in the basement of our shop in Market Street, Manchester. Although I was a pretty successful fashion footwear buyer I knew nothing about the rag trade and bought all the wrong stock. Unperturbed by poor sales, we had fallen in love with the coordinated fashion concept and opened three high street shops in Stockport, Wilmslow and Sale. We employed a general manager, established a dedicated management team with its own Board of directors and lost money at an increasing rate for four years before throwing in the towel. We would have been better spending our time on the struggling shoe retail shops, which, at least, we knew something about.

In the 1980s, with both shoe retailing and shoe repairs struggling against severe competition and facing falling demand, I looked for a new emerging business idea and picked home security – alarms and domestic locks. Another business plan produced a concept we called Security Now, which we started by converting the old shoe repair shop in Lloyd Street, Altrincham and then expanded into the, now closed, Shoetique shop in Wilmslow and an unprofitable shoe repair shop in Stockport. We were lucky to find Darren Pemberton, who knew a lot about locks and did better than break even, but again we would have been better sticking to what we knew.

You may be wondering how a business can diversify if it always has to stick to what it knows best. The answer is to fully understand the kind of thing the business is good at. We survived by realising that our expertise wasn't just in repairing shoes, we were capable of doing any 'blue collar' service on the high street, which is why we were able to successfully bring in key cutting, watch repairs and even mending mobile phones. I now reckon we can claim another skill, the ability to run a multiple chain of service shops, which is why we have been able to extend our business into photo processing and dry cleaning. But we are not qualified to run shops that rely on fashion, we don't know how to run a supermarket and I'm pretty sure we would make a mess of Mothercare, Marks & Spencer, Matalan and Miss Selfridge.

Nearly 30 years after we opened our first attempt at selling security we have managed to establish a successful mobile locksmith service but it took us a long time to work out the secret of that success. After we closed Security Now, Darren Pemberton set up on his own in Oxford Road, Manchester, within yards of the spot where my great grandfather had his first shoe shop in partnership with his uncle in 1865. Once Darren had built an established company he asked me to buy it, which we did, to become the platform to launch a nationwide locksmith service.

The service grew, we recruited some locksmiths, added a network of sub-contractors and set up a call centre at Wythenshawe, but we hardly made any money. The sub-contractors were unreliable and I suspect some of the locksmiths didn't put all the money into the till. We had forgotten what we are good at. We had little knowledge of the locksmith trade but we knew how to recruit people with personality. The answer was obvious: we invited existing Timpson colleagues to change trade and become a locksmith. Several applied, we put them through a four-week intensive training course at Timpson House and our locksmith business is now heading for a profit of £1m a year.

When we bought the Mister Minit chain in 2003 we had to take on Sketchley and Supasnaps to secure the deal. We knew we were out of our depth, trying to run two new businesses, both in rapid decline and providing services which we didn't understand. Luckily, within a year we sold both of them. But by the time we bought Max Spielmann in 2008 we saw the photo business in a completely different light. Despite the decline of analogue photos and the high street recession, we turned Max around because we ran it with the same Upside Down Management model that had been so successful in our core business.

But when my wife Alex took on the challenge of buying The White Eagle in Rhoscolyn on Anglesey to turn it into a busy family-friendly gastropub, we discovered a world of difference between key cutting and watch repairs, and pulling pints. With the addition of The Oyster Catcher at Rhosneigr we found that heated exchanges in the kitchen, a highly seasonal demand and the regulations that rule the food industry were causing us to spend nearly as much management time on two pubs as 1,500 shops. We have now happily merged the Anglesey business with The Crown at Goostrey and The Swan in Tarporley and leave day-to-day management to our partner Woody Barlow, who knows as much about portion control as we know about the use of key blanks.

We are now very wary of being too big for our own boots; we know we can't tell others how to run a business we don't really understand. When we bought the dry cleaning business inside Morrisons and started to add our traditional services we ran them as two separate shops – we didn't want our shoe repairers to go in and destroy a flourishing dry cleaning trade.

The secret is to recognise what you do well – and it can also apply to people. Inspired appointments occur when an individual quality is recognised and used to transform another part of the business. This happened when Janet Leighton was plucked out of our finance department to run the Max Spielmann warehouse on the Wirral. She was an instant hit because someone realised she has a magic touch in managing people. We have many similar examples, like Gouy, our Colleague Support Director, and Darren who oversees our scheme that recruits new colleagues from prison.

It is arrogant to think that you can be successful at running any, and every, business. No one is good at everything, so it is wise to fully understand your strengths and make life easy by sticking to what you do best.

Buy poor performers

If you acquire a highly profitable company you pay a fancy price and find it tough to improve its performance.

Some of our best buys have been from an administrator.

During the last 35 years Timpson has made seventeen acquisitions. That's how we managed to grow from less than 150 shops to over 1,500. But our growth has been achieved while steadily improving our bank balance. The deals that really made a difference were all purchases of poor-performing, poorly-managed companies, most of which we were able to buy for next to nothing.

It is a big mistake for managers of successful companies to think that they can work their magic on any other business that comes their way. Our least successful acquisition was in 2005 when we bought the House Nameplate Company, a well-run supplier of house signs that did an even bigger business with Homebase and B&Q. The price we paid represented a full multiple of past profits and we took on the task of running a completely different type of concern without any clear idea of how to make it any better. It was a naive move: with our attention focused on a fast-growing core business, far from making House Nameplate any better, we helped profits to fall. It is no longer part of Timpson, following a management buyout by my niece, Tina, whose single-minded attention put the business back on track. We just about broke even on the deal but it swallowed a lot of cash and taught us a big lesson. I was saved from a similar mistake in 1997 when I was close to agreeing the purchase of a chain of about 50 watch repair kiosks trading as In-Time, mainly concessions within Debenhams. Luckily for me, the owners pulled out of the deal and I was saved from sinking several million pounds into a venture we knew little about (we had only just started to repair watches at Timpson), with no plan that would have increased their profits.

It is embarrassing to remind myself of the ignorant arrogance

I displayed in pursuing acquisition targets that would do us more harm than good. But at least that experience has taught me that the best deals are done with poor-performing targets, when you have experience of their market and a positive plan for improvement that doesn't rely on much support from your bank manager.

One of the early deals was a good example of a clapped-out company that gave us the chance to make a massive return on investment. The British Shoe Company, which, when we did the deal in 1989, had 28 per cent of the retail shoe market through about 2,000 shops, also had about 50 shoe repair bars, mainly inside their shoe shops. This small shoe repair chain was unloved and badly run but there was one gem – the shoe repair concession in the basement of Selfridges on Oxford Street, London. I offered to buy the business but to remain as a tenant. I devised a commission structure that seemed sure to make money for both of us. We gave them 20 per cent on turnover, but some of the units had a turnover of little more than £250 a week, so, to help me pay the wages, I paid nothing on the first £150 in every shop. We bought the business for £175k with an extra £50k to be paid three years later if we were still occupying the Selfridges concession. The shops made a profit of £250k in the first year and we are still in Selfridges over 25 years later. But we never paid the extra £50k because, by the time it was due, British Shoe was in disarray, the executives who did our deal had all left and no one chased us for the money.

When we bought the 110-shop chain, Automagic, in 1995, although it had gone bust and was in the hands of the Receiver, we had to pay just over £4m to secure the deal. A few weeks after completion I gathered all their area managers together to get their view on why the business had failed. I was in for a surprise

– they thought I wanted their advice on how to improve Timpson by making it more like Automagic. As a result of that meeting all but one of the Automagic area managers left the company, to be replaced by Timpson-trained managers. I had a simple plan: within three months we put the Timpson key cutting system into every Automagic shop – big display, comprehensive training and a few new machines. It cost no more than £600 a shop, but key turnover doubled overnight and total sales went up by 20 per cent. The other big win was in London where nearly all the colleagues were pinching money from the till. We put in two hit teams of experienced and trusted Timpson-trained colleagues who went round the 22 central London shops showing what sales should be achieved. Within a year over half the original Automagic team had gone and sales in London had doubled. In the twelve months before buying Automagic, Timpson made a profit of £400k. Two years later we made £2.5m.

I was starting to realise that turning round badly-performing businesses was a great way to make money, but the secret was to stick to the trade we know, put in our own people to run the new business and have a clear plan that will prove to a group of naturally suspicious new employees that you know what you are doing. During the first few months, trading in a newly acquired company may get worse before it gets better. You will not be trusted by people who have put up with years of poor management and see no reason why the new boss is going to be any better than the last one. Things only really start to improve when they can see that your management is good for their business.

The worst performer we purchased was the UK division of the global service retailer Mister Minit. In the previous four years the business had lost £120m, so it wasn't surprising that we were able to buy the business for a pound. To acquire the shoe repair shops we really wanted we also had to take on two other chains, Supasnaps and Sketchley, plus a number of loss-making Sketchley/Supasnaps concessions in Sainsbury's. Mister Minit, following its acquisition by Swiss bank UBS, had tried to create a new category killer under the brand Minit Solutions, offering a wide range of services, including shoe repairs, dry cleaning, key cutting, watch repairs and photo processing in the same retail environment.

In creating this new brand they made a series of major mistakes, which I mentioned in a previous chapter but are well worth recalling. They spent a lot of money developing a new shop design without realising that in our business it is the shop colleagues, not the shop design, that do the marketing. They saw craftsmen as a liability rather than an asset, stripping shoe repairers from the responsibility for branch management and giving the role to graduates who couldn't even cut a key. It got worse. The established area management team, who had all started as apprentice cobblers, were replaced by executives who had sales management experience with fashion retailers, travel agents and coffee bars. The whole business was heavily controlled by the central team at Maidenhead. When the losses continued to mount and the emphasis was put on cost-cutting, even the dry cleaning branches had to clean their own shop windows and no shop staff were allowed to buy postage stamps. If they needed to send a letter they had to order the stamp from head office, who sent it to them in the post.

We never found a way to make money out of Sketchley or Supasnaps – they were both too run down and we didn't know enough then about dry cleaning or photo processing to give them a lifeline, but fortunately we found buyers for both businesses. The Mister Minit shoe repair shops, on the other hand, were easy to turn round – we simply changed them into Timpson shops. We gave branch management back to the experienced shoe repairers, who were all supported by a Timpson area team, we replaced their poor-margin merchandise with a bigger key cutting and watch repair business and we refitted every shop, changing the fascia to Timpson and giving branch managers the freedom to bring back the window cleaners. Two years later the shops were making a profit of nearly £4m.

There are several advantages to buying a business out of administration. Apart from, quite rightly, transferring the duty to honour contracts of employment, the slate is wiped clean, all debts disappear, property leases come to an end and the new owner has a good chance of putting the business back on a profitable footing. In times of a property boom, renegotiating a complete portfolio of leases can leave the new owner at a distinct disadvantage, but when we bought Max Spielmann in December 2008, the property market was just where we wanted it, on its knees. We were, for the first time I can remember, able to dictate terms to our landlords, who, in a weak market, granted us new leases with a 20 per cent rent reduction plus six months rent-free. With little or no property costs and lots of other savings we were able to recoup the £1.3m we paid for Max Spielmann in nine weeks and had the breathing space to realign the shops from analogue photography to digital. The new Max image made a difference but the real improvement was created by filling the shops with colleagues who rate 9 or 10 out of 10. The acquisition of Max was the first step on a road that has made us the UK's leading high street photo specialist, producing profits of nearly £10m.

Buying poor performers has been an important ingredient in our success.

Keep management accounts off the Board agenda

———— ✕ ————

Put the important topics at
the top of your agenda.

If you give directors lots of figures
they will delve into the detail
and miss what matters most.

O ver the years I've been on lots of committees, governing bodies and the odd quango. Now I'm just on two: our Board at Timpson that meets six times a year and the governing body of our local school, Delamere C of E County Primary Academy, which has a meeting every term. That's a total of nine meetings a year. At one time, wearing all my different hats, I was attending more than that every month – and I don't miss them. But I'm left wondering why some of those meetings took so long (in the late 1970s I was on the National Economic Development Council's Footwear Industry Working Party, which had meetings that took all day), why they often repeated the debate from the previous month and failed to tackle the crucial issues.

Although the person chairing the meeting should guide the discussion, the agenda can keep the talking away from the things that really matter. Standard items to do with governance and risk assessment may divert discussion away from strategy but it is the management accounts that can really hijack the meeting, by giving everyone an excuse to spot the odd mistake and put forward their pet proposals.

Directors with enough time to study the accounts in detail are tempted to take pleasure in publicly pointing out the errors to the finance director. Management accounts give every non-executive director enough information to talk about the business with authority without having any first-hand experience. To some, management is mainly about keeping an eye on the numbers – they talk about 'drilling down into the detail to discover what is really going on' and 'monitoring performance against stretching targets'. I take a different view: running a good business is about people not process.

The figures are made into more of a mystery by finance

directors who compare current performance against budget without any reference to last year. There seems to be a strange view that looking at last year is an old-fashioned habit that settles for an unambitious target. This probably has its origins in the late 1960s when it became fashionable to follow management by objectives and some companies, including Timpson, banned any comparison with last year. I never took any notice then and don't bother much about budget now.

By controlling everything against budget, the finance department put themselves in the pound seats. They set the budget figures so they control the business and depress their colleagues by calling any 'slippage' against budget a major disaster and demanding action to make up the difference and make budgeted profit by the year end. Such comments can be the start of an irrelevant and dangerous discussion. You can't plan profit – any budget is just a guess, a finance director's forecast. I prefer facts to fantasy so I always compare with last year.

Two particular meetings stick in my memory because they showed me how easy it is to ignore the real reason for getting together. The first was a care planning meeting for one of our foster children held at a local school. Although he was one of my favourite foster children he was a difficult child who displayed plenty of challenging behaviour. Alex and I were surrounded by a number of experienced teachers and expert social workers who made us feel that we were the amateurs in the room. It was crystal clear to us that our foster child needed to be moved to a special school that understood how to deal with his difficulties, but the experts couldn't agree. They argued, not about the needs of the child, but about who had the authority to make the decision. After fifteen minutes of posturing between the professionals I interrupted their argument. 'Can I just say something?' I said to startled stares. 'I've been here for some time and no one has talked about Andrew [our foster child]. I thought we were here to talk about his issues, not yours.'

The other defining meeting was when I was a trustee of ChildLine. We started each meeting with a lengthy debate under 'matters arising from the minutes of our last meeting'. ChildLine had a great service but the finances were insecure and the central office lacked strong direction. 'Matters arising' focused on finance and was followed by more talk about cost-cutting under the next item on the agenda which was 'Management Accounts'. It was only my second meeting and 40 minutes had gone by before I said anything. I simply pointed out that we had been talking for nearly three-quarters of an hour and had yet to mention the service that ChildLine was providing to children.

I have never forgotten those two meetings and the way finance and protocol were allowed to take precedence over the main reason we were there. As a result, ten years ago we changed the format of our Timpson Board meetings and put the serious strategic issues at the top of our agenda. Strategy is mainly about the future so we start by discussing all the new ideas that could help grow the business. Then we tackle the day-to-day problems that seem to be getting in the way of greater success, before discussing our profit forecast and future cash flow. We give everyone a copy of the management accounts, but they are in the appendix and before any director goes into the detail, our two hours are up and it is time for lunch.

34

Cash for growth

The time to cut costs is when you are doing well.

Invent an excuse to have a serious search for significant cost savings and bigger margins.

Most management teams believe they run a tight ship with a close control on costs and a strong desire to maximise margins. This drive for profit is demonstrated every year when the company is engaged in compiling the annual budget, with the finance director keeping a check on departmental managers who fight hard for the money to develop their pet projects. Despite politics played during the budget process the finance director usually keeps the upper hand by having a separate set of provisions and setting a pessimistic sales target that keeps costs well under control.

But eventually human nature will defeat even the most tight-fisted finance director. I recommend everyone to read *Parkinson's Law*, a book that reveals why government departments, the European Commission and every business will build a bigger and bigger management team as the years go by. That is why so many people pour into the big City office buildings and fill the corridors of power in Whitehall. It is also the reason why most big corporations have one or two expensive extra layers of management that slow down decision-making and get in the way of people on the front line who make the money.

Normally nothing changes until the company hits a crisis and launches a short-term cost-cutting campaign to solve a long-term problem. I am embarrassed to admit that I've been involved in several of these panic searches for savings which pushed prudence into every corner of the company, cutting the number of office cleaners, cancelling our subscription to the *Financial Times* and even, on one occasion, calculating the monthly use of loo paper per employee. When these superficial attempts at economy failed to improve performance we got round to more serious measures, which usually involved closing shops that we already knew were losing money, and inevitably we made some colleagues redundant and spread doom and despondency throughout the company.

We, like every other organisation, attract extra unnecessary costs as time goes by. We discovered that the best time to have an economy drive is when you are doing well, but needed to find a way to cut costs without instilling negative thoughts of a company crisis. That is why we call our cost-cutting exercise 'cash for growth' – making sensible economies to provide the money we need to invest in the future.

This isn't a team task. 'Cash for growth' is a job for James, my Chief Executive and Paresh, our Finance Director, who start with a simple money-making target of about 1 per cent of total turnover, which makes them look at fundamental changes that departmental managers would find too close to home.

The search for simple but significant profit-making moves inevitably involves some uncomfortable questions. Here are a couple.

Does each colleague do a job that helps the company make money? It takes the annual profit of one of our shops to pay the costs of employing an extra colleague in our office in Wythenshawe.

When did we last check the market to make sure that all our suppliers offer truly competitive prices? Buyers usually claim they get the best prices but experience shows this is seldom true. Whenever a new buyer arrives they always find ways to buy better.

Most cost-cutters begin by studying the management accounts but James and Paresh start their cash for growth exercise by trawling through a big batch of recent invoices, simply to see how we are spending our money. Looking at detailed bills is the best way to unearth unnecessary expenditure, but major savings will only come if you can identify fundamental changes that unlock hidden sources of profit.

Always remember Parkinson's Law ('work expands to fill the time available for its completion'). The costs you are about to cut have probably been created by you and your team over the last few years through the inevitable increase in the size of each department and to fund new ideas that haven't worked as well as you expected. Our cash for growth exercise almost always entails admitting past mistakes.

Think of it as a detox, a slimming regime or a visit to a health farm. Done with diligence, the exercise will make you much fitter – but be prepared to do the whole thing again in three years' time.

Disaster scenarios

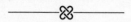

The classic method of risk assessment is a sterile box-ticking exercise that satisfies the need for 'good governance' but fails to fend off the biggest threats to company collapse.

Use your imagination during a pessimistic day, dreaming up your worst nightmares.

The Pensions Regulator expects all scheme trustees to carry out a standard form of risk assessment. This reduces a judgement that needs flair and imagination into a standard process that is unlikely to do any good apart from providing documented evidence that risk has been assessed. The Pensions Regulator is not alone: schools, charities, FTSE 100 companies and no doubt the NHS follow the same formula by rating the impact and likelihood of risk under a number of general headings that fail to nail the real risk. Here are a few risks we are expected to assess – ineffective decisions, inadequate controls, unclear advice and inappropriate investment strategy.

Good governance requires just about every board of directors, charity trustees and school governors to assess the likelihood and impact of up to 50 risk items, adding a few words on how the risk is being managed. As long as the form is completed, agreed by the committee, recorded in the minutes and held on file, the Ofsted inspector, Charity Commissioner and Pensions Regulator are happy. But very little has been done to think through where and when disaster is really likely to strike.

I was fortunate that something similar was being used by the team from Johnsons the Cleaners who were negotiating with us to buy the Sketchley shops in 2004. Their risk assessment incorporated a traffic light system with the results categorised into red, amber and green. After thorough desk research their indicator turned green and to our profound relief, the acquisition got the all-clear. If they had simply spent some time visiting the shops to get a feel of the business, the deal would have been dead in the water with their traffic lights stuck on red.

This risk assessment charade has been around for a long time. Long enough to have predicted the collapse of Barings,

Woolworths and Equity Life. It was, no doubt, an item on the board meeting agenda of every high street bank but failed to forecast and prevent the crisis in 2008. The only people who saw it coming did so by instinct. Process-driven forecasts rely on current trends to predict future performance. For a risk assessment to be worthwhile it must foresee unexpected events by thinking outside the box.

You should have guessed by now that I steer clear of the standard method of assessing risk. I don't debate how we should rate the impact and likelihood of misfortune in 36 specified areas. I simply sit down with an A4 pad and spend a pessimistic but constructive day thinking of the worst things that could happen. By the end of the day I have produced my Timpson disaster scenario that tells the story of each nightmare as it unfolds.

Here are some extracts from the disaster stories I wrote in 2014:

- New EU employment legislation has made it illegal for anyone to work on their own and the latest Working Time Directive brings the maximum working week down to 34 hours with a fine of £10,000 or six months' jail for any breach.

- A new home laser printer has eliminated the need for a photo processing service. This simple device costing less than £30 links to any digital camera to produce high-definition pictures of any size for little more than four pence a print.

- Our ten-year-old small company plane crashes on the way to an Executive Board away day in France, when the pilot has a heart attack. Although no director is killed, none are able to return to work for at least nine months. To cover their absence an interim Managing Director is supplied by a recruitment consultant. After a brief look round the business he makes some major changes to cut costs and tighten management control. His main measures include a dramatic reduction in the size of our field management team, the scrapping of Upside Down Management and an end to most colleague benefits including our hardship fund and birthdays off. All eight holiday homes are sold to boost our cashflow in the face of falling sales as the company starts losing money.

These stories are designed to get my fellow directors talking, not about theoretical risk factors but about the big threats we could actually be facing. It makes us concentrate on the future and the changes that could happen in the world around us. It makes us particularly paranoid about two top questions: Will we be in the right business? Will we have the right people?

All I can confirm is that my maverick method of assessing risk works for us. I don't know whether it would have helped to save any of the companies I have seen disappearing during my years in retailing, like Radio Rentals, John Collier, British Shoe Corporation and Phones4U, but I'm pretty sure it would have made them think about the fundamental dangers that lay ahead.

From my experience it is well worth using your imagination and spending a pessimistic day dreaming up your worst nightmares.

Check the cash every day

It's a thermometer that takes our
daily temperature and reveals
the health of our business.

As long as you control the cash
you are in control of the business.

When Timpson was a subsidiary alongside John Collier, Richard Shops and Allders, as part of the retail group United Drapery Stores, I never bothered about cashflow. To survive in my job as Managing Director I always lived in hope that at least one other part of the group would be performing worse than my bit. Every week we were judged by our sales, each month we had to report profits, but no one ever measured my control of the cash.

When the City press report on quoted companies they concentrate on sales and profit, and are often fooled by some creative accounting that can give company directors the chance to use reserves, exceptional items and 'impairment' to produce a distorted view of profitability. Even the *Sunday Times* Rich List falls into a similar trap by basing its valuations on reported company profits rather than the true ability to create cash and therefore to make money.

A prime example of this sort of naivety has been shown in recent years by the levy charged by the Pension Protection Fund (PPF). Each company pays a levy in proportion to a credit rating, produced for the PPF by Experian. It is all done using statistics that track a range of features including wage levels, type of business and mortgages. Unbelievably, debt levels and cashflow are not included in the calculation. As a result Timpson have been rated as a reasonably high risk. Despite a thick file of correspondence I have not been able to persuade the obstinate civil servants and statisticians that a company with no debts and a pile of money in the bank is at little or no risk of going bust.

My priorities changed as soon we started to negotiate our management buyout in 1983. The management's share of the equity was dependent on having sufficient cash in the business on the date of completion. Suddenly I started to watch the bank balance every day, and have done so ever since. I now know why it is always tougher to negotiate a deal with the owner of a small privately owned business compared with executives in big companies who are not dealing with their own money.

Most management accounts are misleading. Accountants love being in control and keep the rest of the company away from the truth by using provisions and exceptional items or putting certain bits of income or expenditure 'below the line'. The truth is also hidden by those accountants who only compare performance with budget. You can only come face-to-face with the truth if figures are compared with last year.

Too many executives live their lives looking at turnover when it is the margin on sales that really matters. In recent years, retailers have been digging a big hole for themselves, in the run-up to Christmas, by putting on cut price events and making a big thing of Black Friday at the end of November. I remember the happy days when you sold everything at full price while customers were in a buying mood, before clearing slow-moving stock in the January Sale.

I detect a similar obsession with price among online retailers. With little chance to provide a true personal service, price comparison is seen as the main way to attract internet shoppers. It certainly works. Armchair browsers can easily spot a bargain and, as we have found on our Tesco photo website, cut price deals bring a big boost to sales – but they don't always increase our profit contribution.

In the 1990s, shortly after I had acquired all the other management shares and became 100 per cent owner of the company, I commissioned our daily cash report. I realised that I was only truly in control of the business if I had control of the cash. It wasn't long before I found that, on its own, a simple statement of our bank balance was fairly meaningless. It came to life as soon as I added a comparison with the exact same day last year and the figure we predicted on the previous day.

A short email told me a lot about the business and prompted some pertinent questions. Was the figure worse than yesterday's forecast because of lower turnover or an unexpected payment to suppliers? Is the figure worse than last year because of lower profits or high capital expenditure? It is always good to have money in the bank but even with an overdraft, if it is less than last year, you have evidence that the company is creating cash.

Despite this daily company health check I still experienced a few surprises. The worst was when I was boarding a plane en route for a fortnight in the Caribbean in January 2004. The business was struggling to digest a major acquisition. In 2003 we bought the UK arm of Mister Minit that included two other chains, Sketchley and Supasnaps. Both were making a loss and our attempts to put them back into profit were soaking up cash. Sitting in my seat before the plane took off, I got the daily cash report – it was suddenly nearly £2m worse than I expected. The seatbelt signs went on before I could ring the office for an explanation and I spent the next nine hours imagining a future full of doom and gloom. In Barbados airport I got an email that showed the situation wasn't as bad as I feared: the scary figures were more due to the timing of rent and tax payments, rather than trading getting desperately worse, but the episode underlined the value of taking the temperature of the business every day.

I learnt another lesson. The bank balance tells you a lot, but it doesn't reveal all you need to know. To get the whole picture you need to take account of all your borrowings – and the finance department can massage the figures by delaying payment to suppliers. We've fixed the payment problem by always sticking to our contracts (I disapprove of those bullying suppliers who dictate new terms to suppliers when it is too late for them to argue). To give us the whole picture our daily report also includes the total company borrowings, which, of course, are compared with the same day last year.

As the years go by we get more obsessed with our cash position, still looking at it every day but also looking ahead by month, by year and even in a decade's time. We are lucky to have found acquisitions and projects that provided a rapid return on investment and run a business that creates cash nearly every week of the year and only needs a modest amount of capital expenditure.

I confess that the same financial prudence doesn't extend to my own financial affairs. I can't remember the last time I looked at a personal bank statement, but I have nearly all my money invested in the business and I know that as long as I'm in control of the company cash I have control of the business.

Learn from mistakes

Management schools can't teach you as much as you learn on the job.

The biggest lessons are learnt when you make mistakes.

The biggest benefit of the strong business partnership I have with my son James is the way he is able to learn from my mistakes. He has the humility and wisdom to ask me the key question: 'Can you ever remember anything like this happening to you?' I was able to ask my father and grandfather a similar question so James can tap into the experience of three previous generations, demonstrating one of the key strengths of a family business.

My grandfather taught me a lot about property. He built a fabulous high street portfolio in the 1930s but most of his advice was based on the few failures rather than his many successful deals. 'You will never make money on The Moor in Sheffield', he told me, 'the rents are too high and the customers have little money to spend.' His advice, based on opening a loss-making shop, held good in the 1970s and 80s when I foolishly followed in his footsteps and opened two loss-making shops on The Moor.

It is easy to get it wrong in the property market. The high street is always changing and every new shopping development is a gamble, but the big mistake made by the Timpson property team that succeeded my grandfather after the war, was to take small shops in low-income neighbourhood centres when they should have had the courage to take much bigger shops in the city centres. Playing safe doesn't always work. Consequently Timpson shoe shops lost market share and we were overwhelmed by the British Shoe Corporation (Dolcis, Saxone, Manfield, Freeman, Hardy & Willis, Trueform, Curtess, etc.) who treated Britain's streets like a monopoly board, building shoe shops wherever they could. We have learnt a lot from that experience in the last twenty years, taking our shoe repair business away from second-rate shopping streets and opening in the busiest bit of town.

You can learn a lot from the mistakes made by other people. My biggest lesson was observed at John Collier, the tailor, where I was working for a few months in 1973. The management team were cock-a-hoop, having produced a record year with their memorable advertising campaign grabbing customers from all their main rivals, including Hepworths, Burton and Weaver to Wearer. But while they were celebrating success the John Collier team seemed unaware that the market was changing dramatically to their disadvantage. Over 90 per cent of their sales came from made-to-measure suits, but within a decade ready-to-wear clothing had taken over and by 1990 the John Collier name had gone from the high street.

That episode taught me that nothing is for ever. Businesses can't stand still – they have to adapt in tune with changes in the world around them. Shoe repairing was in a similar position to made-to-measure suits; we could not afford to stand still. But one of my earlier retail experiences taught me another big lesson. Just because you are good at running one business doesn't mean you will do well at something entirely different.

Experience shows that many ideas that seem sure of success fail when they are put into practice. When I was helping my father with the washing up we usually talked about business and I learnt much more from this than I was taught during three years getting my degree in Industrial Economics. I was excited when he said that if we could just sell one extra pair of shoes per day in every shop we would double our profit. But he then went on to explain that this type of claim is totally naive. The discovery of a statistic won't increase turnover and profit – you need to find the way that will attract new business. Since that conversation over the kitchen sink in about 1957 I have seen several plans that have included the assumption, 'If we only sell one extra item per branch per week'. I have learnt to ignore the maths and wait for reality to tell the truth.

I made a similar naive mistake in 1997. The business was going well but I thought we were losing sales due to low staffing levels in some of our high-turnover shops. I thought our bonus scheme was to blame. The sales target for each shop, each week is set by multiplying the wage cost by 4.5 and the bonus is split between the colleagues according to their skill level and the number of hours they worked during the week. There was a big incentive for the colleagues to work on their own and I convinced myself that many were failing to serve every customer in their quest to maximise bonus earnings. My answer was what I called a 'free man' scheme, with 50 shops selected to have an extra colleague without it being charged into the bonus calculation. I was in for a shock. Instead of bringing a big boost to business, my free man scheme actually reduced sales! With a spare person hanging round, much of the buzz disappeared from the shop and the more laid-back atmosphere was bad for business. My clear logic didn't, in practice, add up to common sense, so I scrapped the scheme, saved the extra wage cost and sales went back to the former level.

There is one area where bitter past experience is often forgotten. The saying 'once bitten twice shy' doesn't apply to people who are blinded by technology. The dotcom bubble around the millennium should have put off the majority of the investing public, but in 2017 they are still happy to invest in companies with a high market capitalisation and no chance of making a profit for many years to come. I was sucked in by the magical mystique of the internet in the fairly early days (about 1999) when I was persuaded that we could make money by keeping a record of customers' car keys on computer and for an annual subscription promise to rescue them at the roadside if they lost their key or locked it in the car. The plan, which we called KeyCall, was to have a network of computers capable of copying the required keys and a team of motorcyclists on call to come to the motorists' rescue. It got worse – we spent several thousand pounds on market research focus groups which produced a positive approval of the scheme and proved without question that there was a substantial demand. Riding on a wave of unthinking enthusiasm, I agreed to a direct marketing programme using leaflets tucked into the middle of several Sunday papers. After eight weeks only ten customers had signed up to KeyCall, including two colleagues from our office who were testing the system and an aged aunt who was trying to do me a favour.

The trouble with a lot of this new technology is that few of us are willing to admit that we don't understand it, but don't be fooled like the crowd watching the emperor in his new suit of clothes. I hope I have now learnt that it is best to stick to projects you understand.

The most difficult lessons to learn are all to do with people. Most of us are keen to give poor colleagues a second, third and even a fourth chance, although we know it is highly unlikely that they will change their negative personality to produce a positive performance. Remember that over 85 per cent of most management's time is spent dealing with people who are pretty useless. We kid ourselves that the latest recruit to our senior management team found by an expensive headhunter will produce a miracle within months. But nearly all our experience shows that new blood is more likely to make things worse and within eighteen months you will be working out the least expensive way to part company.

Mistakes should be cherished – every one is part of your learning experience. Be thankful that you know you have made an error; some people go through life making the same mistake not knowing they are doing anything wrong. Making mistakes can help you become a better manager and sometimes a major crisis can lead to a new way of making money.

In 1971 our shoe shop on Grove Street, Wilmslow had a serious fire. When we reopened the shop ten days later for a Fire Sale there was a 50-yard queue and we achieved three months' sales in three weeks.

That experience taught me how to run a sale. When we closed the whole of the Timpson shoe shop business for two days to prepare for our July Sale in 1975, and advertised on television that we were shut, we had queues all over the country. In three days we beat our best-ever Christmas week takings. I used the same technique some years later when we closed all 110 Norvic shoe shops. Over a period of six months we closed about six shops a week, always shutting each shop on a Saturday night and starting the sale the following Friday morning at 10.00am. The results were spectacular, with sales reaching between ten and twenty times the average weekly sales in the first nine days. To accommodate the crowds we cleared out all the customer chairs, displayed the stock on racks and kept a queue for as long as we could by simply letting in eight customers at a time. It became a well-oiled routine which never met a problem until we came to shut the Norvic shop in Windsor, situated just across the road from the castle. The manager refused to change the way he served his customers. 'Windsor people expect a proper service even in a sale. They must be able to sit on a chair and be served by a member of staff using a fitting stool.' We ignored his plea and said the chairs had to go,

despite his last-ditch argument: 'What about the one-legged customers?' We closed the shop on the Saturday night and Windsor
folk showed the same enthusiasm as elsewhere. A long line had
formed ready for the sale starting the next Friday. Right at the
front of the queue was a man with one leg.

Fortunately our current business has no need for a sale, but I
guarantee that if you have a lot of old stock to shift, close the shop
for at least two days before the sale begins. If you don't believe
me, look at Next.

And a final thought: there is probably some truth in the saying that there is no such fool as an old fool, and I admit, even
people over the age of 70 make mistakes. But you are never too
old to learn.

Summits

—⊗—

Put your top performers together
and get them talking.

There is no need to use outside
consultants when you employ
a business full of experts.

I'm often asked how we developed our watch repair service or what we did to develop the skills to fix mobile phones, and most people are surprised by the answer. We needed expert help to get started. Our first watch repair training was done by a couple of experts with a lifetime's experience in the trade, then we sent loads of colleagues to a residential seminar at the British Horological Institute near Newark. Our initial introduction to mobile phone repairs was inevitably guided by teenagers and tech superstars in their early twenties (my fifteen year-old grandson was providing a service repairing phones and tablets for fellow pupils and staff at his school, before we ever offered the service on the high street).

Once outside experts had taught us the basic skill we did the rest of the training ourselves. Few highly qualified watch repairers also had the personality to serve customers and boost turnover. Keen cobblers and key cutters, having seen the potential sales and bonus to be earned from repairing watches, were quick to learn new skills and build up an extra source of business. As soon as we had a hard core of our established colleagues who were providing a proper service, we used their example to train the rest of the company.

Every day I get several emails from companies offering advice on how we can improve our business – some even say that they have the ultimate secret to our future success – but I've always found the best ideas come from colleagues inside the business rather than outside advisors.

With a team full of colleagues who are trusted with the freedom to use their initiative, individual shops are full of good ideas which have the potential to improve the whole of our business. In our Upside Down Management world, instead of new initiatives being dictated by management most of our innovation starts from the shop floor, though managers must spot the best ideas and spread them round the company. That is why they hold what we call summits.

A summit is a brainstorming session where we gather together up to ten internal experts to talk about their specialist subject. The topic might be mobile phone repairs, dry cleaning, training or how to organise an area social calendar. The participants aren't picked according to their status or position in the management structure; we try to find star performers with the most knowledge, the best ideas and the ability to talk. Many don't realise why they do so well until they chat with like-minded experts and discover what it is they have in common.

Two hours should be quite long enough. You are there to listen, but, at the start, you need to welcome the participants, introduce the topic and get everyone relaxed. Be patient, it could take time and you may need to work hard to get the conversation going, but, if you have picked the right people, it won't be long before they are immersed in their debate and you can keep quiet and take notes.

Prepare a list of questions in case the conversation runs out of steam or strays too far from the point and fails to include some of the areas you want to cover. But don't dominate the discussion. There is little purpose in plugging your pet theories or pushing your point of view. Just keep your opinions to yourself and allow your front-line experts to reveal the secrets behind their success.

Successful summits spread new ideas and increase your knowledge about the business, but they do something else: they give you the opportunity to spend time with some of your best people, who will have been proud to be picked to give their expert opinion.

Chairman's Report 2032

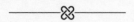

*If you've already seen something
in your dreams, you are prepared
when it becomes a reality.*

**Get in a time machine and
send your imagination
on a mystery tour.**

In 1985, I took my senior management team for a three-day discussion in Stratford to produce our business plan for the next five years. I still have the report, which makes somewhat sad and symbolic reading. Each manager outlined their department strategy, which dovetailed into the master plan that produced a dramatic improvement in profits. But when I looked at the detail, not much had changed, apart from the sales which were forecast to rise faster than costs.

The plan never worked out in practice. Two years later, the shoe shops were heading for a loss and we sold the company. I now know that you can't plan profit. That was the last time I produced a five-year plan. We have a cash prediction based on existing trends, but when it comes to long-term planning I do it in an entirely different way.

Traditional business plans usually show success by predicting that the business will do whatever it does now but do it better. But past experience shows that our future success will almost certainly depend on new ideas and how well we can manage change.

A small number of significant events changed the fortunes of our business. When we had a boardroom bust-up in 1972 and my father was fired as Chairman I didn't realise that this catastrophe would turn out to be one of my biggest lucky breaks. The introduction of key cutting in 1969 started the transformation from cobbler to multi-service shop. Each acquisition has made a massive difference, especially our first major move when we bought Automagic in 1995. The purchase of Max Spielmann in December 2008 had never been on our radar until they went into administration. Just over three weeks later we had 200 photo shops and photo is now our company's biggest service. The first pod we opened outside Tesco in Warrington, in the car park next to Warrington Wolves rugby league stadium, was an experiment that transformed our property portfolio – we now have over 200 pods with many more to come.

Few of these things would have been predicted on a Board retreat and that meeting in Stratford could never have contemplated our development of digital identity, mobile phone repairs and the Timpson website. Next year our watch repair business will be bigger than shoe repairs and we didn't repair our first watch until 1996. Our ability to introduce new ideas and adapt to change is so important that I have invented a completely new approach to forward planning.

Every so often I put myself in a time machine and write my Chairman's report for fifteen years in the future. I picked fifteen years because that is far enough ahead to allow your imagination to break free from the present but close enough to keep in contact with reality. The Chairman's written report is the perfect format for storytelling, which I hope comes through in the following extracts from the report I wrote in 2014 for our 2029 Annual Report:

CHAIRMAN'S REPORT 2028/29

During last year we celebrated the 125th anniversary since repairing our first shoe. It is, therefore, a good time to look back at the remarkable events of the last fifteen years.

Upside Down Management

Despite the dramatic pace of change we have consistently stuck to what we do best. Timpson continues to concentrate on service retailing in the British Isles. Apart from a short spell in 2015 when net borrowings reached £4m, the business has always been in funds and with no bankers or outside shareholders insisting on nit-picking governance or 'best practice' we have been able to use common sense and keep clear of red tape.

Our trade mark, Upside Down Management, has developed dramatically over the last decade and the new book *We All Work Upside Down* has been in the top ten bestselling business books for the last 79 weeks.

Regular leadership courses help us keep our unique culture and we have maintained a continuous crusade to only employ colleagues who rate 9 or 10 out of 10. Some years ago we were told by several bigger companies that our type of delegation would only work in a modest-sized business. We have proved them wrong – the secret behind keeping in close touch with 15,000 colleagues and giving freedom to each individual has been the promotion of ten key superstars who James picked to run the main strands of today's Timpson. It's vital to appoint managers with the right personality, who can take responsibility and delegate authority. We have a senior team who truly 'get it'.

Max Spielmann

After twenty years of sparkling success, Max seems to be heading towards another period of uncertainty. Sensor photography and Morton technology could be changing the way we take and store pictures, threatening Max on the high street and its links online. However, passport photos and ID, the major contributor to photo's £350m sales and £49m profit, looks like having a further boost now that the government has approved the upgrading of our vault to store the latest biometric holograms which meet international standards. Early moves to accept selfies with passport applications in 2017 were scrapped after a faulty auto-recognition scanner mixed up Robbie Williams with Ed Miliband. The upgrading of our vault will almost certainly ensure that we will continue to be the preferred ID supplier to all the main banks, the Post Office, casinos, nightclubs, liquor stores and the Premier League.

Timpson Tech

Developed out of our phone repair service, Timpson Tech is rapidly becoming the nation's technology helpline both on and off the high street. With most Tech colleagues under 25 and several 16-year-olds who work in the school holidays, they call themselves the Grandparents' Advice Bureau.

It is amazing to think that originally most of our sales came from repairing broken screens on mobile phones. We soon found that repairs to tablets, game consoles and laptops gave a better margin so the range of jobs expanded. Today, with all household appliances controlled by computer, Timpson Tech is swamped answering day-to-day problems and customers are happy to pay for the advice.

Timpson Tech still has a nationwide branch network but most of the advice is given over our online video link, based at our tech excellence centre, with support from a fleet of mobile techies (although many of our most knowledgeable colleagues aren't old enough to drive!).

New Services

Each year we look at a large number of new opportunities but few fit into our business model. We still intend to concentrate on high-margin service businesses that give colleagues the opportunity to earn a big bonus.

Although our men's hairdressing experiment never made money, the ten nail bars we have opened in supermarket car parks seem to fit our formula and could become a national chain. The picture framing part of Snappy Snaps is being introduced into Max and we have a prototype 'party shop' that uses our personalisation skills to provide everything from party invitations to banners, balloons and decorated cakes.

When asked why he picked nail bars, James said: 'I didn't fancy a tanning studio, tattooing, dog grooming or dentistry.'

Prospects

With economic cycles taking about twenty years, 2029 is proving a more difficult year. However, despite the falling house prices, high unemployment and rumours of problems in the banking sector, we continue to operate in markets that are relatively resilient in times of weak consumer spending. We have had plenty of good news from the bad weather; since 2023, when scientists finally confirmed that the globe is no longer getting warmer, we have seen a succession of typical British wet summers and an increase in demand for traditional shoe repairs.

Whatever happens in the next twelve months our success will still depend on having a business full of people who rate 9 or 10 out of 10 and giving them the freedom to do their job the way they know best.

My forward-thinking fantasy Chairman's report generates a lot more relevant discussion about future prospects than I've ever experienced from producing the more conventional type of five-year plan.

Agree with your customers

———— ✗ ————

*Outstanding organisations provide precisely
what each individual customer wants.*

**The right answer is,
'Yes, we can'.**

At Timpson, we don't have a marketing department. Our last press advert was placed in 1988, a three-week campaign to push shoe repairs in Scotland that succeeded in increasing turnover by less than 1 per cent. Since then I've only been tempted to put money into marketing on one further occasion. I have been a Manchester City season ticket holder for over 25 years and when we moved from our old ground, Maine Road, to what is now called The Etihad, our seats had no view of a scoreboard. I took the initiative and wrote to the Man City Chairman who sent a polite reply promising to raise the matter at a subsequent Board meeting. Nothing happened so I wrote again and got nothing apart from another polite reply; so I sent a cheque for £25 made out to the 'Manchester City scoreboard fund'. That did the trick. Within a week a member of their events team came to my office and I quickly agreed to fully fund a new scoreboard at a cost of £53,000 on condition that it displayed the word TIMPSON in big letters for the next three years. I'm not sure whether it brought in more business but I could now see a scoreboard and had cemented a warm link between my business and my football team without having to buy an expensive seat on the Board.

Although we don't advertise in the usual way by taking space in newspapers, television or websites, I reckon we advertise over 400,000 times every week. Every time we serve a customer we are promoting the business, for good or bad. The best way to build your reputation is through the recommendation of existing customers and the best way to get their approval is by giving them the service that they really want.

I am well aware that the customer isn't always right. We get a few pompous, ignorant, rude and sometimes dishonest customers who would do us more good by going down the road to pester our competitors. But over 95 per cent of shoppers are genuine, decent and honest. The rules that some companies introduce to prevent being exploited by rogue customers can irritate the majority of people who deserve to be trusted and be given exactly what they want.

In the 1990s I realised that sophisticated electronic point of sale tills were getting in the way of great service. They gave head office the opportunity to take control of the shop floor and caused countless shop assistants to tell their customers, 'I can't do that, the till won't let me'. I can't be the only shopper who has a string of stories about how the cash register ruined my customer experience.

Fairly recently back at my favoured football club, Manchester City, I was entertaining four guests. Before the game we ordered a round of drinks – two pints of lager, one white wine, a Diet Coke and a glass of tap water. When the girl came back carrying a tray of drinks, the tap water was missing. 'Sorry', she said, 'we can't serve tap water, there isn't a button for it on the till.'

Some years ago I was in the Malmaison hotel in Edinburgh. After a busy day visiting our shops I went into the bar, ordered a pint of beer and got some good news: 'It's happy hour', said the waitress. 'You can have two for the price of one.' So I changed my order to two pints, started the *Telegraph* crossword and considered myself lucky that I had placed my order at 6.55pm, just in time to qualify for the special deal. But I was in for a disappointment, as the waitress returned carrying a tray with just one pint. 'Bad luck', she said with the hint of a smile. 'By the time I put your sale through, the clock clicked on to 7.00pm, Happy Hour was over and the till wouldn't let me pour the second pint.'

As I spend a lot of my time travelling the country visiting shops I usually pick up snacks and lunch from bakers and coffee shops. One day, in Gosport, I popped into the bakers three doors away from our shop to buy a doughnut. 'Please can I have a jam doughnut?' I asked. 'We only sell them in packs of five', said the counter assistant. 'Look at the display, that's what we do.' I tried to be helpful. 'I really only want one doughnut, but if it helps I will buy two.' 'I don't think you understand', insisted the assistant. 'They are packed in five and the till only lets me sell five at a time.' I gave up and bought my doughnut from Greggs.

Although I'm a regular customer at Greggs I sometimes have a problem making my usual purchase, a portion of soup. It was fine before they introduced a special take-out bowl for soup, which might work for an office worker sitting at their desk but doesn't do the job when you are driving round in a car. I need my soup in the cups they use for coffee, but I don't always get what I want. 'I can only serve soup in the proper container', I was told at one shop. 'It is company policy.' And at another I was told it was 'Due to Health and Safety'. To be fair, after a bit of a battle, most Greggs assistants serve me my soup in the way I want.

I recently bought a shirt from my favourite, but expensive, shop, Etro. Sadly it didn't fit (either the shirt was too small or I was too big). I went back and found a replacement which was £25 cheaper. I was given a credit note. Perhaps I should have been pathetically grateful that they had taken back my ill-fitting purchase, but, having spent a lot of money at Etro over the last five years, I felt the credit note was small-minded and inappropriate. But the manager wouldn't budge: 'Those are the rules laid down by Head Office in Italy and I have no option.'

My favourite story of inflexible service that puts company policy in the way of customer service comes from Kerry, our training supervisor, who was living on his own and went shopping for swedes. At his local Sainsbury's he spotted a special offer

— 'Free swedes if you buy 5lb of potatoes'. Kerry had plenty of potatoes in stock, but he was passionate about swedes. He took a packet of swedes to the check-out. 'Where are the potatoes?' said the assistant. 'I don't want potatoes, I just want swedes.' 'But you can't have them without the potatoes', said the assistant. 'I'll pay for the swedes', said Kerry. 'You can't pay for them, they're free', said the assistant. 'But I don't want them for nothing! You tell me how much they are and I'll pay for the swedes.' 'Sorry, can't do that.' Exasperated, Kerry found a supervisor who allowed him to buy the swedes for the price of a packet of potatoes.

If you want to amaze customers, agree with what they want and deliver a service way beyond their expectations. It is simple and obvious: you can't create a loyal customer base by making every purchaser stick to your rules. When they are in your shop it is their shop and they expect to get whatever they want in the way they want it. People go back and do more business with suppliers that make them feel special.

If a customer starts the conversation by saying, 'Could you possibly help me by ...', or 'I don't suppose you can ...?', the answer in every possible instance is 'Yes, we can'.

I love it when our colleagues surprise their customers with unusually great service. It is often the little things that make a big difference:

'I'm a bit worried whether your original key will create a proper copy. Take the keys home and check they are OK and then pay me when you are next passing our shop.'

'Let me look after all those bags while you finish the rest of your shopping and I will have your shoes ready when you get back.'

'Of course you can take your child upstairs and use our loo.'

'Let's open the packet of laces and try them while you are

here. I don't want you to go home with something that is of no use to you.'

These are all words that have caused customers to write personal letters to me praising the service they have received. Agreeing with customers and giving them all they want and more is a marvellous way to build a reputation.

But, however nice you are to every customer and whatever you do to bend over backwards in their favour, you will still have customers who insist they are getting a raw deal.

I'm not naive, there are a few professional complainers who enjoy pointing their finger at honest traders by dishonestly claiming unfair treatment. I remember in the 1960s when the first moulded soles for men were marketed with a six-month guarantee, some mates managed to share the same pair of shoes and if one was on night shift they were able to wear the shoes for nearly 24 hours a day!

But most complaining customers honestly believe that they have a real grievance, so it is always wise to give the benefit of the doubt. Whatever you decide to do following a complaint, do it quickly – tardy complaint procedures can cause more irritation than the original problem. If a customer sends me a personal letter or email I always find that the best thing to do is pick up the telephone and talk it through with them. Most are surprised to find that it's the Chairman on the phone.

We have improved our business by trusting our colleagues to use their initiative and in turn we encourage them to trust their customers and give them a service that goes way beyond their expectations.

If you agree with your customers there is a strong chance that they will love your business.

Be friends with everyone

*It's so much easier to do business
with people you like.*

**As you go through life, make
friends rather than enemies
– next time you meet you
might need their help.**

During my career I've met many people who think managers, to be effective, should be tough and aggressive. Competitors are the enemy and should be treated with contempt. Customers are treated with suspicion and must be made to stick to the rules. Suppliers are squeezed until they hardly make a profit and employees are kept in their place with strict rules and belligerent bosses.

When I started work in 1960, employees certainly got a raw deal. No living wage, working time directive, equal pay or maternity leave. In those days pregnant women were more likely to get their P45 than time off work. There was a massive gap between the boardroom and the shop floor – separate dining rooms and cloakrooms, executive parking bays and much longer holidays for senior executives.

Legislation has created a much more friendly workplace but a macho mood still exists in the mind of many managers, who treat business as a battle, with customers, suppliers and competitors all batting on the opposite side. Some of the tactics they use give business a bad name.

Customers, who should be seen as the company's best friend, are forced to follow a set of rules, either announced on big notices: 'No £50 notes', 'No refunds', 'No children', or craftily included in paragraphs of small print. Some shops seem to be run on the assumption that every customer is a criminal and no one should be trusted.

Some big businesses treat their suppliers as a punchbag to be pummelled into submission whenever sales and margins suffer. Binding contracts are ignored when defenceless suppliers are told to make a 'special contribution' to help their big brother customer pay for a poor period of trading by knocking 3 per cent off all the prices and providing an extra 28 days' credit. This business bullying is no way to build the trust needed for a long-term commercial relationship.

The contempt for competitors can get unnecessarily confrontational when one competitor is doing a deal with another. Sharp practice, disguised as smart negotiating ploys, has never impressed me. I know that adversaries who are always 'in a meeting' and don't reply to emails are doing it deliberately and I'm not surprised when the same party tries to chip the price just when we are ready to exchange contracts, but in the long term these smart tactics seldom seem to do much good. The best deals for both sides are done between like-minded people in a civilised manner.

I have always thought it odd when other executives suggest that you should never allow two members of the same family to work together. We have lots of shops run by husband and wife, mother and daughter or father and son, and it nearly always works well. So well, in fact, that we give an incentive of £200 per placement to anyone who successfully introduces a friend or relative as a new Timpson recruit. Our record so far is eight members of the same family working for the business at the same time. It is so much better to have colleagues who are on the same wavelength and enjoy friendship at work. As long as they come with the right positive personality, the more friends and family on the payroll the better we seem to do.

Nor do I subscribe to the idea that managers and their junior colleagues shouldn't socialise outside work. Some companies foster a 'them and us' atmosphere by discouraging friendships across the management structure. I just think that is off-hand and unhelpful. We might pay managers more money but in all other respects they are of equal status and I hope they find everyone friendly, whatever job they do.

No manager can be a truly great boss if they don't know the people in their team. It isn't enough just to know what the colleague does at work; to really understand what makes each colleague tick, it is important to know about their home life and their hobbies. It helps you to help them with any problems they face and gives a guide to how you can award exceptional performance.

I spent several years buying ladies' fashion shoes for our shops and would have found the job much more difficult if I hadn't had the help of a number of true friends. I shared an office with Tom Hardman, who bought the more basic footwear for women, and Tom Howell, who was responsible for all the children's shoes. The two Toms were at least 25 years older than me and massively more experienced. They could have resented this young family upstart who had been parachuted into a fairly senior role and expected to be taught all the tricks of the trade. Far from being miffed, they took me in hand and gave me a great grounding in how to be a buyer. We became firm friends.

Two other people who became both tutors and friends were suppliers and also close competitors of each other. John Hirst, who made fashion shoes in Waterfoot, in Lancashire's Rossendale valley, and Bill Taylor, his rival from Bacup, just down the road, proved to me the value of being friends with someone who is selling to the same customers. At least once a year the three of us went together for a week in Italy to look at the shoe shops in Rome, Florence, Bologna, Verona, Padua and Venice. They taught me how to spot the styles most likely to sell at home twelve months later and introduced me to some remarkable restaurants.

This wasn't the traditional supplier–buyer relationship with the manufacturer picking up the tab at every turn. We had a kitty and enjoyed each other's company. Together we built a big and successful business.

John Hirst and Bill Taylor gained a lot from their friendship and we too have benefited from keeping in close touch with our competitors. I first met Ted Adler, who owned a well-run chain of service shops called Essex Shoes, in 1988. After a few years I introduced Ted to my son James who kept in close contact with him and, I think, impressed him with the way we do business and look after our colleagues. When Ted decided to sell his shops he sold to us, and I hope he still feels he made the right choice.

Being Mr Nice Guy makes a lot of business sense. It can't be a good idea to go through your career picking up enemies. You never know who you are going to meet again in the future – but you can be sure that if you made a black mark it won't have been forgotten. Opportunities often come because of who you know, rather than what you know, but you won't be given a chance by someone who owes you no favours.

It is much easier to do business with people you like and can call a friend. If you find friendship difficult it is probably a sign that they don't get your approach to business. But even if you come across a person you find tricky and not easy to respect, be pleasant and claim the moral high ground by staying calm and, if they show their true colours, refuse to sink to their level.

Always remember that good business isn't created by putting in the perfect process – it is all about people, and it is so much easier to do business with people you like.

Trust your intuition

*Leadership is about having a vision
and getting everyone to follow you.*

**Great entrepreneurs base their
best decisions on experience,
flair and common sense.**

My first executive role at Timpson was as the buyer of ladies' shoes for our shoe shops, and it was a great preparation for the decision-making part of management. At first I was naive enough to think it was possible to develop a set of guidelines based on past experience. Looking at the best and worst sellers for the last ten seasons I developed my set of rules which included: 'Don't buy two-tone shoes', 'Ankle straps never sell' and 'Only buy a limited quantity of white shoes'. Although all these statements fitted our past experience, within three years I had discovered that they offered disastrous advice, especially when we had a summer season when every woman wanted white shoes with ankle straps. Shoe fashion follows a twenty-year cycle, from pointed toes to big wide toes and back to points, and along the way lots of unexpected twists and turns emerge. My university degree in Industrial Economics had trained me to analyse facts to predict the future, but I had been given a job where decisions purely based on data didn't work.

Of course the past was important, but to be a successful buyer I had to keep ahead of the minds of our customers and anticipate what they would like in twelve months' time. I learnt to trust my own judgement and make bold decisions based on my feel for future fashions. Perhaps that experience made me into a bit of a maverick manager who has always relied on intuition ahead of safe statistical analysis.

As I mentioned in an earlier entry, the last time we used a shop design consultant was in 1994. After a four-hour meeting with me, when I told him all I knew about the business, he visited ten shops and returned with his initial proposal. First he gave his overview on our business, which was little more than telling me what I had told him at our first meeting. Then he produced his big idea – to use a different colour for each of our services (at that time we did shoe repairs, key cutting and engraving). I paid him off with £5,000 for the time spent and went to Bath where I took a picture of every shop I liked the look of. Back in the office I pinned all the photos on the wall and picked out my favourite, which is how we decided on a shop design that has lasted for over twenty years.

A lot of other retailers use marketing consultants to help analyse new shops. I prefer the Ken Morrison approach of going out in the car and 'looking to see where the chimneys are'. During the last few years many of the newly opened supermarkets have failed to match their sales forecast, despite, no doubt, being based on expert research evidence of the spending power and social economic profile of those living nearby. To me, deciding whether you should open in a particular site is similar to the way I picked my range of shoes nearly 50 years ago. Never mind what the figures say, the most important factor is how you feel – if it doesn't feel right, don't go there.

Elsewhere in this book I describe how we pick our colleagues – no psychometric assessments, not much bothered about qualifications or comments on the application form, the only thing that really matters is the interviewer's impression of the candidate's personality.

Throughout my marriage I was given a masterclass in the power of intuition. Within weeks of meeting Alex I was struck by her confident, clear thinking and was amazed to discover that she had passed only five O Levels (the equivalent of GCSE). This was why I made a stupid remark, meant as a compliment, that nearly ended our relationship only a few weeks after we first met: 'What you lack in intelligence you make up for with common sense!'

Alex never kept any credit card receipts, she never looked at her bank balance and seldom bothered to get a second quote if she liked the person that gave the first one, but she had an amazing intuitive insight when it came to the big choices in life.

Three decisions, driven by Alex, stand out from the many bits of inspired advice she gave me during nearly 50 years. Alex was the one who always had faith that the management buyout would work, and it was her faith that drove me to work incessantly for nine months to make it happen. In 1989, Alex stopped me floating the company, a move that would have inevitably led to oblivion; and two years later Alex encouraged me to take out a £1m mortgage to buy out all my fellow shareholders, a move that gave James and myself the chance to create the unique culture that defines Timpson today.

The rapid growth of our business has been helped by a series of acquisitions, mostly from a receiver or administrator. To outsiders I have no doubt that many of the deals have appeared extremely risky, but I never had doubts about any of the deals we have done. We reduce the risk by knowing the business really well – we had been looking at these companies and their shops for years before we made an offer. We never use a merchant bank; we do the deals ourselves and base our judgement on intuition, but the more you know about the business the better your best guess is going to be.

Intuition came to my rescue in the middle of the night when we were finalising the deal to sell Sketchley to Johnsons. Johnsons' Chief Executive, Stuart Graham, had us up against the ropes. We were desperate to sell a company that was using up a lot of cash and he enjoyed being the macho negotiator. Gradually we gave ground and agreed just after midnight to drop the acquisition price to £1, but Stuart Graham still asked for more. He wanted us to include the Sketchley concessions in Sainsbury's supermarkets which had never been part of the deal. We refused because the concessions made money and I somehow thought that it was important to maintain our link with supermarkets and have dry cleaning as part of Timpson. Keeping those sixteen concessions has helped us build a dry cleaning service which has played a leading part in developing nearly 400 supermarket concessions.

Alongside intuition it is also helpful to get a bit of luck. It would have taken us a lot longer to realise the true potential of our watch repair service if it hadn't been for a visit from H. Samuel, the jewellery chain. We were meeting to discuss a possible engraving contract between a Samuel shop and their local Timpson. 'But', said Samuel's marketing manager, 'there is a problem. We have just seen your shop in Yeovil, where you are doing watch repairs. We have a watch repair turnover of over £13m and wouldn't want to deal with a competitor.' That was all I needed to know.

Leadership is about having a vision and putting it into practice by getting everyone to follow you, but just because you are the leader, don't assume you are the only person with good ideas. Go and talk to people throughout the business who are full of suggestions which they also base on intuition.

Be yourself

You can't be an expert at everything;
know your limitations.

The business will reflect your
values, so stick to your beliefs and
stay on the moral high ground.

Sometimes I am asked, 'How can I become an entrepreneur?', perhaps in the hope that there is a book that can transform any individual into a copy of Sir Richard Branson. It doesn't work like that. Budding entrepreneurs need a good commercial idea and the spark of ambition. Without the raw ingredients no business management school or executive coach will turn a competent middle manager into a tycoon.

But I don't mean to be pessimistic, there are plenty of people who have the full package – brimful of ideas, overflowing with energy and the perfect personality to be a leader. They can learn a lot from experience, pick up a few lessons from streetwise friends and senior colleagues, and even benefit from talking to a life coach. But business is not a game like *The Apprentice* – you are not taking part in a play, it isn't theatre. This is the real thing and true leaders are true to themselves.

Be realistic: most, if not all, of your team are better than you at the jobs they do. You can't be an expert at everything; the only thing that matters is being good at running the business and supporting your colleagues.

Don't try to become a stereotype, because there isn't one. Successful entrepreneurs come in all shapes and sizes, they are driven by their individual dreams and seldom follow the herd. They do it their way.

You don't have to go to conferences or trade association meetings just because that is what other executives do. Networking can be an important part of the job but you are more likely to find useful contacts at events you enjoy. Despite being a pretty keen golfer, I desperately dislike corporate golf days.

There is nothing worse than spending the whole day on a round of corporate golf, which usually starts with a bacon sandwich at 9.45 before the first four tee off at 10.30. You don't get on the course until 11.20 and two hours later are still playing the eighth hole, hoping that a big bird will swoop down and pluck you off the fairway and fly you back to your office. Back in the clubhouse at 4.00 you still have two further hours to kill, talking to the same strangers you met on the first tee, before dinner is served sometime after 6.00. Despite having a hopeless round yourself, you feel duty-bound to stick around for the prize-giving and contributing to the raffle before leaving for home at 8.45.

Allow yourself to be entertained by all means, and do some of the entertaining yourself, but don't go to Test matches, the opera, Six Nations rugby or the Chelsea Flower Show unless it is something you want to do. Although Alex complained that, by planning the diary, I was wishing my life away, I firmly believe that making lists of the things you need and want to do and putting cherished dates, particularly holidays, in the diary is a necessary way to keep control of your life.

I am wary of the amount of time that can be soaked up by visits to London. I have got to like London, but in reasonably small doses. Twice a month is about my limit. But I have to be firm. I come across a lot of people who assume that either I live in London or, when they discover I don't, think it would be a thrill for me to get on the train at Crewe and spend a whole day to attend a 90-minute meeting near Moorgate. I was once approached to do a television news interview and was asked where I live. 'Cheshire', I replied. 'Is that near London?' asked the researcher. 'No', I replied. 'We have another studio in Croydon', she said, presumably hoping Cheshire wasn't far away from Surrey or Sussex. After a bit more geographical information she came up with the answer: 'We've got a mobile unit up north, I'll get them to pop round to you.' It never happened – she thought it would take their team less than an hour to get to me from their base in Newcastle upon Tyne.

Don't let yourself down by copying the bad manners that have become commonplace in business. I can't stand dealing with people who don't reply to emails, are always in a meeting, always on voicemail, take four weeks to reply to letters (civil servants please note), and think lying is a perfectly proper tactic to use when you are negotiating a deal. Thankfully I have got to the stage, and the age, when I don't need to do business with people like that. I get so much more enjoyment from dealing with nice people whom I respect, because they know how to behave.

Never be afraid to show your ignorance. If there is something you don't understand, ask – you may well be asking questions others didn't have the courage to raise. It is good to be paranoid. Paranoia is the perfect way for an optimist to avoid complacency. I can assure you that it is possible to be both optimistic and paranoid. If I didn't worry as much as I do about our future, I wouldn't feel as optimistic about our chances of success.

Your business will reflect your personality. People follow the boss's example in both what they do and the way that they do it. Your colleagues deliver the day-to-day performance but you set the strategy, create the culture and display the standards of behaviour that others will follow.

Be yourself and set an example that puts you and your business on the moral high ground.

Have a social conscience

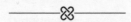

Making money isn't the only objective.

**Don't tick other people's
socially correct boxes:
faithfully follow the principles
that really matter to you.**

It is fashionable to adopt a politically correct agenda, which, today, includes fair trade, conservation, a responsible carbon footprint, no discrimination of any kind, and no gender pay gap. We follow all these aims – and by repairing shoes can be said to be a green business – but none of this is what I mean by having a social conscience.

Having a conscience isn't simply a question of following worthy objectives, it is much more personal than that. To be socially responsible you must be faithful to the principles that really matter to you.

In running a business you take on some major responsibilities, not just to the shareholders but also to all your suppliers, neighbours, customers, even your competitors and particularly your workforce and their families. To put everything into perspective, compile a list of all the people whose lives are touched by your business in the course of any one year. What you do, and the manner in which you behave, can make matters better or worse for the world around you.

If you are fortunate to head a profitable business that creates more cash than it needs, you are in a privileged but awesome position. You have the resources to support causes beyond your immediate business world and make a difference in the wider community.

These are all rather grand words and high ideals that may get many readers nodding in agreement, but they mean nothing unless a business and especially its Chief Executive has his or her own social conscience and the will to make things happen, starting with the way company colleagues are treated.

No employer should underestimate the significance the company has on the lives of its colleagues. We have several members of the same family working at Timpson, parents who trust us so much that they encourage their children to join our payroll, and partners who both work for us, thus relying on our business for all the income that comes into their household.

Every Timpson colleague wears a badge. Under their first name, and a chosen tag line, is the date that they started working for us. For example, it says 'Part of the Family since 2006'. A company with a social conscience must see its colleagues as the top priority, part of an extended family. We look after our own people before thinking of giving support outside the company. Upside Down Management means that every manager's main role is to support their team by being a good listener and providing sympathetic advice. We are there to help when things go wrong, writing letters of condolence, helping to unscramble a debt problem or going along to a divorce court to support a colleague fighting for access to their children. We don't like politics and have no favourites; every Timpson colleague is of equal importance and they all deserve to be part of a company that cares.

But having a social conscience doesn't mean being a soft touch. It is vital that we preserve a sense of community. Our colleagues spend a huge slice of their waking lives at work, so it's our responsibility to ensure that they are part of a happy workforce – that is why our job includes helping colleagues who let the team down to find their happiness elsewhere as nicely, as generously and as quickly as possible.

Sometimes we are described as philanthropists, but we seldom give any money to charity. We are much more likely to give our time to further a cause that we believe in. James spends at least one day a week helping to improve our prison system in his role as Chairman of the Prison Reform Trust, networking to get more companies to employ ex-offenders, and trying to secure much-needed changes to the way prisons are run.

Much of my time is spent helping adoptive families and looked-after children, particularly by widening knowledge of 'attachment theory' in schools to help children with behavioural problems receive a more appropriate education.

James and I are lucky. We both have the time and money at our disposal to make a difference to causes close to our heart, but the real heroes and heroines are the colleagues who act as carers, bring up disabled children, work at local youth clubs or coach a junior football team every Sunday morning. They are precisely the sort of people you want to have sitting at the next desk or working in the same shop.

You may well wonder what all this has to do with shoe repairs and key cutting, and a few years ago I would have felt the same, but I have now seen the value of having a business full of like-minded people who are at ease with themselves. It makes a massive difference when you have a business packed with good, outgoing personalities who respect other people and receive their respect in return.

Recently someone, hearing about our company culture for the first time, asked whether our family has a faith – I think he assumed we were Quakers or were following in the footsteps of Lord Leverhulme. But I had to disappoint him. Despite being taken by my mother to Sunday School I have no strong religious faith, but I do believe that having a social conscience is also bloody good business.

45

Have a company charity

Make a practical as well as a monetary contribution.

Choose a cause close to your heart that both your colleagues and customers can support.

Alex couldn't resist the invitation we received from the Duke of Westminster to join him for a private dinner at his home, Eaton Hall. It was an enjoyable evening, held to launch the NSPCC Full Stop campaign in 1999. 'I suppose you realise that we never spent a penny', said Alex as she drove the car home. 'What are you proposing to do to help their campaign?'

I found it difficult to get to sleep, wondering what to do, but by the morning I had the answer. 'Bits of stitching and holes in belts', I declared to Alex. 'What are you talking about?', she asked, before I revealed my idea to raise money for the NSPCC.

Our shoe repair shops have always responded to a number of small requests – stitching, glueing, holes in belts and a number of other odd jobs – by doing them for nothing. My idea was, instead of saying, 'That's no problem', we would say, 'Just put a pound in the box' – and collect the money for the NSPCC.

It worked. Customers embraced the idea and we regularly collected over £3,000 a week, which was increased by the money Timpson colleagues raised from a number of sponsored runs and charitable events. I soon realised the added benefit of having a company charity – it provides the perfect answer to the begging letters we receive from all the other worthy causes it would be impossible to support.

After two years I felt we were ready for a change. Despite being one of the best known charities it was difficult to explain exactly what the NSPCC did with the money, and on top of this lack of focus I found them somewhat dictatorial, especially when their London head office insisted that we submitted all display material for their approval. I let area managers decide our next company cause and was pleased that they picked another children's charity in ChildLine. By now we were raising an average of £4,000 a week which meant we were big enough and ChildLine was small enough for us to matter and make a significant difference.

After about six months Esther Rantzen, founder and Chair of ChildLine, asked me to be a trustee and I started to realise how much more a company charity means if you are directly involved rather than simply sending money. As well as attending the trustee meetings I also went to several of their call centres, sitting in on training sessions and listening to calls as they came in. Esther in turn showed an interest in our business and met many of the Timpson colleagues who were helping us raise the money.

ChildLine was our company charity until, with my encouragement, it was merged with the NSPCC, who had much stronger finances and central support. The merger strengthened ChildLine and gave the NSPCC a highly respected service that I believe has become its star performer. By then I'd already met Lynn Charlton, the Chief Executive of the Manchester-based charity After Adoption, and was starting to fund a support programme for adoptive families called SafeBase, which became our next company charity. The money raised through our shops is used to subsidise local authorities who provide SafeBase support to local families.

By then, we had started to organise all charitable activity through the Timpson Foundation which was guided by Helen, our financial controller, Alan Brown, former governor of Liverpool Prison, Alex, my son James and myself. In addition to SafeBase, we set up a chefs' academy at our pub, The Oyster Catcher on Anglesey, where we helped young people from the island with multiple barriers to employment.

Our most far-reaching Foundation project started in 2002,

when James was visiting Thorn Cross, a prison near Warrington. Matt, the inmate who showed him round, was so impressive that James gave him a business card, saying: 'When you get out, give me a ring and I will find you a job.' Matt is still with us, a successful shop manager who is one of over 400 ex-offenders who now work for our business.

By specialising in the recruitment of people from prison we have found plenty of star performers whom other employers had totally ignored and we have set an example that other companies are starting to follow. The respect James has gained as the leading employer of ex-offenders has been admired by both our colleagues and our customers, an unexpected way to enhance our company's reputation.

Our fourth major project started as an attempt to save a local primary school which was threatened with closure. As part of the rescue package at Delamere County C of E Primary, where several of our foster children were educated, we set up a bursary of £150,000 over five years to provide extracurricular activities that broadened the range of education and opened the children's eyes to the wider world of possibility. It worked – the school was saved, then flourished, and is now an academy filled to capacity.

We only take on new projects in which we can be directly involved and make a significant difference. The latest challenge is to help refurbish and revitalise a lads' club close to our office in Wythenshawe that had originally been established by my great uncle Noel Timpson. Several of our colleagues have volunteered to plan and oversee the development.

Colleagues often raise money to support our company charities and the company regularly gives money to causes supported by colleagues. Some colleagues even organise their own fundraising events, like Keith Bergum, manager of our Timpson shop in Birchwood, who ran a series of golf days to raise money for Home Start, in memory of Alex, my wife.

But the most important part of our Foundation is the work we do to support the colleagues themselves. Our hardship fund usually provides loans to about 20 per cent of Timpson colleagues to help with short-term cashflow problems, and every month there will be some special circumstances that we help to resolve by paying a bill or buying a much-needed item of furniture. When deciding where the money goes, our colleagues are always the top priority – charity always begins at home.

Sit down with an A4 pad

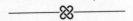

In a bath or on the beach – great ideas appear as a flash of the obvious.

A pen and A4 pad make it much easier to think.

At the end of my *Desert Island Discs*, having picked eight records, I had to choose a luxury to take to the island. I was keen to have a tennis court, with a robotic opponent, perfectly programmed to keep me fit and steadily improve my game so, when I was rescued, I would be a match for anyone. I was hoping that this luxury would include a pen and paper, not just to record the score but also so I could write a novel. I wasn't allowed to do both, so I abandoned the tennis court and picked an endless supply of pens and A4 pads as my desert island luxury.

On the island, I would have plenty of time to write that first novel, but, in business, it is difficult to find the time to think. Some executives try to clear their minds by retreating to a distant hotel for a forward-planning conference, but so much time is spent checking emails and contacting the office that the group have little chance to concentrate on the future until late at night when a free-ranging discussion takes place in the bar.

I never found a company retreat particularly productive. It might enhance team spirit but I find it easier to dream up our strategy in the peace and quiet of my own home. To me the Chief Executive and the Chairman make the key strategic decisions, the rest of the team are consulted, but they only really get involved when the plan is put into practice.

I'm happiest sitting in my study, with no noise, a view of my garden and an A4 pad. I have always been a list-maker. Some people more meticulous than me (like Manchester United ex-manager Louis van Gaal) write down every detail in a big notebook; I prefer an A4 pad for my list of ideas and things to do. But the biggest benefit I get from pen and paper is the ease with which they help me make decisions and create our strategy.

With no one else watching I can scribble any thoughts,

however bizarre. Ideas are best written down before they are forgotten. They may not necessarily be in a sensible order, but having a random collection of pertinent thoughts is a great way to get started. Sometimes I draw diagrams or cartoons instead of writing, as it is often easier to think in pictures rather than words.

I like using the simplest technique to make a decision. In deciding whether we should start repairing mobile phones or how I should vote in the EU referendum I simply made a list of the reasons for and against. Usually the issue is made clear by an overwhelming number of reasons to decide one way or the other.

A4 pads have played an important part in all the big decisions that have been critical to the growth of our business, from our management buyout in 1983 to the purchase of the Tesco photo business in 2014. My toughest decision was the sale of our shoe shops in 1987. Although the list of reasons for staying in foot-wear retail was far outweighed by the list for getting out, I still had to overcome my sentimental attachment to the part of our business started by my great grandfather in 1865. It was an A4 pad that made me put emotions to one side and face up to reality. The same A4 pad technique demonstrated the game-changing potential of our purchase of the Automagic chain of 110 shoe repair shops in 1995 and gave me the courage to, for the first and last time, totally ignore the advice of my wife Alex.

Sitting down with a blank sheet of paper helped me ana-lyse deals and discover critical factors that are seldom revealed by an accountant's spreadsheet. Most transactions aren't just about numbers – the secret to success usually lies in spotting the opportunities that others cannot see. In 2008 we toyed with the opportunity to buy Persil Services, which consisted of about 50 dry cleaning and photo processing concessions in Sainsbury's supermarkets. To many it would have seemed a strange thing to do. Half of the outlets were part of the package we had sold to Persil Services in 2004 and others occupied spaces we had abandoned in 2003 when closing a lot of the loss-making concessions we inherited from Mister Minit. To make matters worse, the Sainsbury's executive for concessions was giving our Chief Executive James a hard time by using impolite and bullying bargaining ploys.

Although everyone else, understandably, was wondering why we should bother to deal with a combative Sainsbury's executive just to get a loss-making business, I remained positive. Four years before, we had kept our best sixteen Sainsbury's/Sketchley concessions out of the sale to Johnsons the Cleaners and my A4 pad analysis told me to buy Persil for the same reason. It would give us a significant platform on which to build a dry cleaning service and extend our business out of town. Looking back, it was definitely the right call.

These days I spend a lot of time using an iPad and an iPhone, but despite all the support on offer from consultants offering computer-based analytical advice, my most useful decision-making tools remain a pen and an A4 pad.

Recognise stress

Alternating between misery and butterflies in your stomach, stress makes you turn trivial problems over and over in your mind.

Then, suddenly, you wake up one morning and it's gone.

Plenty has been said and written about keeping fit, the importance of work–life balance, regular exercise, proper holidays and the ability to relax. People cycle to work, others do yoga, join a gym, play tennis, practise Pilates – all hope that this will help to keep them fit, both physically and mentally. Some, despite following a sensible routine and looking the picture of health, can still suffer from stress. I know, it has happened to me many times. It's not your fault, you haven't done anything wrong, it's just the way you are.

It first happened in about 1976. I had been running the Timpson business for about a year and everything had gone well; sales were well up, our profitability was outperforming many other parts of the UDS Group and I enjoyed being busy, but perhaps I got a bit complacent. My honeymoon period was bound to come to an end. Unseasonal weather brought a few weeks when sales were poor, stock levels rose, and some poorly judged buying meant more markdowns than usual, so profits would suffer. Within days I turned from the perfect optimist to a glum pessimist.

Suddenly I was spending every waking moment turning problems over in my mind. Mostly they were things that didn't matter that much. Trivial decisions that would normally never have bothered me now took on great significance. I was worried about everything but couldn't make a decision on anything. Any sense of priority had disappeared, all areas of my life at work and home assumed equal importance and I felt unable to cope. My days were spent between periods of real misery and times of nervous despair – either unhappiness or butterflies in my stomach, nothing in between.

I remember the morning when I was at Macclesfield station, waiting for the train to Euston. I looked round the platform at my fellow travellers: some in groups heading to a trade fair, two, wearing business suits, in deep discussion interrupted by laughter. Wherever I looked people were happy and animated, looking forward to their trip to London. I was envious, wishing that I could swap my mood for theirs. While they were laughing and joking I was worrying about my day ahead. I was going to a meeting of multiple shoe retailers. I had read the papers, distributed ahead of the meeting, but couldn't concentrate, so I didn't know what they said. I was nervous, the butterflies were back and I didn't fancy facing a room full of people, so I spent the next few minutes trying to decide whether I should abandon the trip. The train arrived, I found a seat and started to worry about something else.

One of my biggest worries was me. I was scared to tell anyone about the way I felt, worried that others would realise that I was as inadequate as I now believed I'd become. I just hoped this dark period would disappear, but every morning when I woke up it was still there. I was yet again going from nervousness to misery, and even before getting dressed I was worrying about the latest insurmountable problem. I didn't even tell Alex, but she knew, it wasn't difficult for her to notice I had changed and it can't have been easy for her to live with the world's most perfect pessimist. She chose her moment and got me to talk, then told me to go to the doctor.

Just talking about it helped a lot. Dr Angus Luscombe, in Wilmslow, explained how stress can happen when the normal fight-and-flight instincts that equip us to deal with the stresses of life get to breaking point. But he gave me some happy pills and the good news that I just had to be patient and it would go away. He was right – the chat in itself made me a bit more positive and three weeks later I woke up without a care in the world.

He didn't tell me that stress would return, but when it did at least I knew what it was. I have had many of these dark times when stress takes over every moment of your thinking day. Some bouts are a lot worse than others and there doesn't seem to be any particular reason why. Surprisingly, I had no problem coping with two of the most stressful times in my life, when I was involved for nine intense months negotiating our management buyout, and during the months after Alex died.

Alex got to know the signs, she even detected the early indications of a new period of stress before I did. She insisted I always sought help from a doctor, telling me: 'Don't just sit and sulk, do something to help yourself' – and she made sure I told Christine, my PA, and our close family. 'They need to know why you're so moody.' Sometimes the pills didn't seem to do the trick and I had some counselling sessions combined with a number of bizarre relaxation techniques (don't ask!) but I still don't know what works best. All I do know is that stress, for me, has a happy ending – the magic day when you wake up and everything is back to normal.

I've included this chapter on stress because I have discovered it helps to talk about it. It helps me to understand myself, but I have found it is helpful to other sufferers to discover they are not alone. When it first happens you think that you are the only person in the world who has ever faced the problem. It is a relief to know you are normal, perhaps a bit unlucky to be made that way, but totally normal in the way your body is behaving. The worst that can happen is for you to keep quiet about it, and the first step on the road to getting better is to tell your close family and friends, then go to see a doctor.

I also hope this chapter will help those people who never

have had, and never will get, stress symptoms. It may explain why some of their very best colleagues suddenly become withdrawn and indecisive. They may be reluctant to talk to anyone but hopefully when the time comes you will be a good and sympathetic listener. Stress is often caused by the pressure of dealing with other people, but the support of colleagues can be an important part of a speedy recovery.

Have a mentor

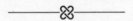

Running a business is a lonely job, but you don't have to do it on your own.

Mentors don't tell you what to do, but their support helps you make the right choices.

A chief executive is responsible for supporting everyone in the business but no one is there to support the chief executive. It can be a lonely role and if you are a worrier, like me, you can spend a lot of time turning over difficult decisions in your mind without coming to any conclusion. We all need to talk, but there are some things that you can't chat about with your immediate colleagues. That is when you need at least one mentor.

There may be no need to pay for a professional life coach. You have probably got a close friend who knows you and knows a lot about your business, someone who will listen while you pour out your problems and a person you trust to give good guidance and keep the conversation confidential. The chance to talk is so much better than grappling with hard decisions on your own, and advice can carry much more weight when offered by someone with no axe to grind.

There are times when it helps to have a mentor who is also a work colleague. I usually have a few branch managers whom I trust to keep me abreast of the shop floor gossip. It is the same in the office; it helps to know colleagues who can confidentially tell you what you need to know. If you sense a feeling of unease it is good to talk to someone with their finger on the pulse. The girl on reception or the man in the postroom may well provide a better perspective than your senior managers.

I have an old-fashioned view of the role played by non-executive directors. Institutional shareholders expect their non-execs to concentrate on governance, keeping management on a tight rein and minimising risk. I want non-execs who will act as a sounding board, providing moral support and encouraging a thoughtful but positive approach to new projects. Patrick Farmer, who was one of my non-execs for nearly twenty years, was the mentor who helped me plan my son James's progress from management trainee to Chief

Executive. Patrick wasn't just a mentor to me – his advice was also trusted by Alex. We both needed a wise advisor who wasn't part of the day-to-day team, and Patrick was perfect for the job. He even understood the tricky side of me, as Chairman, being married to the Chief Executive's mother.

I've been helped by a number of mentors. Lawyer and non-exec Roger Lane-Smith masterminded my management buyout and voiced the art of possibility that gave me the determination to pursue several more important deals that sometimes seemed unlikely targets. Corporate communications advisor Michael McAvoy taught me how to see things from other people's point of view and helped me get a positive reputation for customer service. Using Michael as my guru I made communications and PR a central part of my Chairman's role. These days I have a mentor called Brian Thompson, who seems happy for me to talk out my business problems over a round of golf. Like every good mentor he is a sympathetic listener with loads of patience.

The word 'networking' is usually associated with a constant search for new customers or future recruits, but the biggest value that comes from new friends who work elsewhere is the supply of new ideas and the chance to talk to people facing similar problems. For over a decade James has played an active part in the Young Presidents' Organisation (YPO), which has been both his mentor and his business school. The YPO, with a membership confined to chief executives under the age of 50, produces powerful support, by putting lively like-minded high achievers together in groups that encourage the exchange of personal experience. By joining, James discovered a network of knowledge provided by a multi-talented collection of mentors.

It can help to have different mentors for the various parts of your job, and, indeed, for the non-business bit of your life, but too much advice can be confusing. Even if you ask for advice, the final decision is always yours. Mentors mustn't tell you what to do, they are there to help you make up your mind. Don't get upset if you disagree with some of their ideas – you won't always see things the same way. But if you are regularly coming to opposite conclusions, it is time to look for a new mentor.

Good mentors act as a sounding board, they are an extra source of ideas and a second conscience. Sometimes they can be challenging by playing devil's advocate, but they should always both test and build your confidence. You should always feel better about life after meeting your mentor.

For most of my life I have been fortunate to live with my main mentor. During our first few years together, Alex watched my career carefully and kept pretty quiet, but she was taking it all in and when I needed her help she knew exactly what to say. In the background, Alex took control when I was reeling from the bust-up that led to a boardroom coup and the firing of my father. Alex never wavered in her faith that our attempted management buyout would finish in success. For much of the time Alex didn't want to talk about business. She didn't need to know about the record weeks or the war stories that ended in triumph by beating a competitor; she wanted to keep my feet firmly on the ground, but could read my moods like a book. Her mentoring was reserved for the tough times when she could clear my jumbled mind and put her finger on the real problem and a realistic solution.

My most important mentoring took place in bed, chatting over a morning cup of tea, and, although Alex died in January 2016, she is still my major mentor. If faced with a tricky problem the key question I now ask is, 'What would Alex have said?'

Spend plenty of time with your family

All work and no play makes Jack a dull boy – and it isn't good for your business.

Don't miss out – children grow up remarkably quickly.

My children should be writing this chapter, not me. I'm sure they spend much more time with the family than I did when they were young, but thank goodness I did take some notice of Alex when she told me: 'If you don't make time for the children you will miss them growing up and before you know it they'll be gone.'

It just took me a bit of time to learn. When Alex and I got married I was working long days during the week and played sport all weekend. Golf on Saturday and Sunday morning, and, depending on the season, cricket or hockey in the afternoons. When we got married I stopped the Sunday afternoons and when our eldest, Victoria, was born I gave up the Saturday morning game of golf. When James was born I cut out the hockey and cut down on cricket, especially after Alex made it clear that she would not be willing to join the team of wives providing tea between the innings. When Edward was born, golf became more infrequent but I took up squash at Alderley Edge, very near home, so I could return home in little more than an hour.

Although Alex rightly claimed that I could have done more, I have albums of pictures to prove that I did my share of the Saturday shopping with one, two or three children in tow, Sunday afternoon walks in Styal woods, hours spent on the touchline at Wilmslow watching mini rugby, and on the boundary for Terra Nova cricket. In the early years our holidays were in the UK, usually North Wales, Devon or Cornwall, then we discovered camper holidays in the USA, teenage holidays on the Algarve, and skiing. People didn't talk much about work–life balance in those days, but looking back I can see how much my time with the family put work into its proper perspective.

I was lucky: because Alex persuaded me that we should

become foster carers, I have been surrounded by young children for most of my life – we had over 40 consecutive years when we had to have babysitters every time we went out for dinner. I attended a lot of carol concerts and nativity plays, queued patiently to listen to loads of teachers at parents' meetings, took many boys to Cubs and one girl to Tai Kwando, and I learnt as much as they did along the way.

But from what I see today, many busy executives find more time for their family and are all the better for it. I'm not trying to defend my generation but I do think that modern business is better equipped to bring families together. The internet makes a big difference if used in the right way. I used to have a really tough time when I went back to work at the end of a holiday; it was probably one of the main causes of my stress. Inevitably I would have left a lot of problems behind – the holiday wasn't just a chance to spend all my time with the family, it was a way of escaping from the pressure of work. But, in truth, there is no escape and on my return there was a massive file of papers to tell me that none of the problems had magically disappeared. I don't have that difficulty any more, as emails keep me in constant touch. In the early days Alex tried to ban my BlackBerry but I simply hid it in my washbag. Eventually she realised that you can have a much better holiday when you know what will be waiting for you back home.

The internet helps in an even bigger way: it gives nearly everyone the chance to benefit from flexible working. You don't have to be in the office to keep in touch. Mobile phones help me to spend more time going round our shops and the internet lets me work at home.

But not all of the latest technology is family-friendly. Ready meals in front of the television and constant contact through Facebook and Twitter have cut right through family meals, the perfect time for everyone to sit down and talk. But you can't talk to a teenager who is talking to someone else on Twitter.

Our Sunday lunch was always a big deal, especially during the seventeen years when my mother-in-law joined us every week. Sometimes as many as twelve of us would be there and Grannie – surrounded by grandchildren, her daughter, son-in-law and some foster children – would lead the conversation and supervise the table manners. She would have been horrified at the idea of tablets at the table or ringtones interrupting the conversation. If ever James came round, in the latter days with his children, we were under strict instructions not to talk about business. Even in a family business, the business and the family need to keep their distance.

For a family business to survive there needs to be someone from each generation who has both the talent and the personality to lead the company and make it better. It helps a lot when one generation gets on well with the next. We have been fortunate. James and I have enjoyed a particularly fruitful partnership, which is helped by knowing each other so well. James seems to have an uncanny ability to read my moods. I know that James is very like his mother. If we disagree, I let him win.

The time you spend together as a family influences your life today and helps to keep you close to your children for decades to come.

Keep it simple

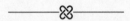

Don't waste time on things that don't matter.

**Great managers make a
complicated business seem simple.**

Life is pretty complicated and our business is probably more complicated than most. We employ more than 4,500 people in over 1,600 shops doing shoe repairs, key cutting, watch repairs, engraving, dry cleaning, photo processing, passport photos and mobile phone repairs, and we put plenty of holes in belts. In addition we have 60 mobile locksmiths, seventeen separate dry cleaning hubs, an engraving centre near St Helens, a watch workshop in Wolverhampton, a specialist shoe repair centre inside a prison near Warrington, a key cutting call centre in Wythenshawe, a central photographic workshop on the Wirral, a mobile technical team servicing 700 self-service photo machines in 280 supermarkets, 32 area teams, two warehouses and an office.

Life became a lot easier when we introduced Upside Down Management. It was so much less complicated when we didn't have to tell everyone what to do. With every colleague trusted to look after the routine, we are free to concentrate on the strategy and keep a close eye on the culture. It is often said that retail is detail, and I can't imagine how anyone can run a multiple chain without constantly visiting the shops. But every business needs a boss (perhaps both a Chairman and Chief Executive) who can stand away from the detail and see the big picture, the things that matter most for future success. There is no reason why customer-facing colleagues or line managers should be bothered about cashflow, capital expenditure or management succession, but they are top priorities for the boss.

There is no point in wasting time on things that don't really matter. Don't feel you have to read every trade magazine that is freely delivered to your door. Delete any email that invites you to a breakfast meeting, seminar or webinar. Don't go to a meeting unless you think your presence will make a big difference, and never become part of a standing committee that doesn't know when the time has come to stop meeting.

Have you noticed how much time some people spend arguing little points that are a minor part of a big deal? Here is my advice: don't bother, let the other side have their way, just concentrate on the terms of the deal that really matter.

If you don't know how to solve a problem, do nothing. Sleep on it, wait until the answer appears, possibly in a flash of the obvious that suddenly shows you the way. On the other hand, don't continue to turn over the pros and cons of a situation when you've already decided what to do. If you know what to do, get on with it and do it now. Simple.

Top 25 Phrases

1. As long as you control the cash you are in control of the business.

2. Have a business full of characters who rate 9 or 10 out of 10.

3. If it doesn't feel right, don't do it.

4. Management is an art not a science; break the rules, but stick to your principles.

5. Great companies have great people.

6. Don't waste time on things that don't matter.

7. Every time a weak colleague leaves, you strengthen the business.

8. Money isn't the only objective.

9. The time to cut costs is when you are doing well.

10. Always find time to look after your star performers.

11. You can't be an expert at everything; know your limitations.

12. The more rules you have, the less important they become.

13. If you can't trust your colleagues you must be picking the wrong people.

14. Cut across the management structure and talk to everyone.

15. You can always find an excuse to have a party.

16. It makes a big difference when journalists talk to the boss.

17. The best praise isn't part of a process, it comes as a total surprise.

18. Get colleagues who run your business to tell you how well the business is running.

19. In a world full of social media, the best form of communication is still meeting face-to-face.

20. It's so much easier to do business with people you like.

21. Some of our best buys have been from an administrator.

22. The best way to say 'well done' is with a proper pen in a letter sent to the colleague's home address.

23. Over half the things that will make us money twenty years from now have yet to be invented.

24. People find it easier to read pictures rather than words.

25. The right answer is, 'Yes, we can'.

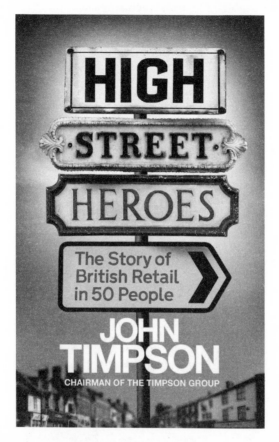

High Street Heroes:
The story of British retail in 50 people

When businessman John Timpson started his retailing career
in 1960, there were no supermarkets, no out-of-town shopping
centres and not even a hint of internet shopping. The British
high street was full of made-to-measure tailors and traditional
grocers. Timpson shows how forward-thinking shopkeepers and
inspirational entrepreneurs have led the major retailers through
a period of rapid change – people such as Ken Morrison,
Ralph Halpern, Terence Conran and Anita Roddick, without
whom our high streets would have looked very different.

978-184831-916-5
£12.99

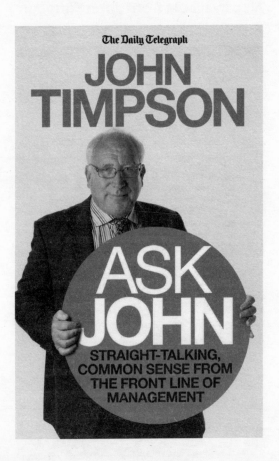

Ask John: Straight-talking, common sense from the front line of management

John Timpson's *Daily Telegraph* column, 'Ask John', has been dispensing straight-talking, no-nonsense business advice for more than five years. This book collects and expands the very best from that column for the first time. From why low cost will never be a real substitute for proper customer service to the etiquette of employing interns, John's honest, common-sense business advice should be required reading for anyone running a business – whatever the size.

978-184831-789-5

£12.99